Singles Ministry
Can Change
the World

Fernando Alejandro

ILLUMINATION PUBLISHERS

Singles Ministry Can Change the World
Copyright © 2022, by Fernando Alejandro

ISBN: 978-1-953623-93-5. Printed in the United States of America by Illumination Publishers, wwwipibooks.com.

Unless otherwise indicated, all Scripture references are from the Holy Bible, New International Version, copyright Γ1973, 1978, 1984, 2011 by Biblica, Inc. Used by permission. All rights reserved worldwide.

Cover design by Roy Appalsamy of Toronto, Canada. Interior layout by Toney Mulhollan.

Our books may be purchased in bulk for promotional, educational and theological training use. Contact Illumination Publishers International at IPinfo@ipibooks.com.

The views or emphasis of the author are his own and do not necessarily reflect the views of Illumination Publishers.

About the author: Fernando Alejandro came to faith in June of 2000 in the Pioneer Valley Church of Christ in Western Massachusetts. Fernando would go on to lead the singles ministry there, and later would oversee the singles ministry in the One Miami Church in Miami, Florida along with his wife, Rosa Alejandro. In addition to these ministry roles, Fernando helped organize a teacher's ministry group within the Pioneer Valley Church and has contributed to the teaching and preaching functions at both Pioneer Valley as well as the One Miami Church. Fernando is pursuing his Masters of Divinity at Gordon Conwell Theological Seminary. Fernando can be reached at ofpowersandcrowns@gmail.com.

www.ipibooks.com

Table of Contents

PREFACE

Several years ago, a small group of single disciples gathered to talk and dream about their respective singles ministries. The singles stage of life had born in us an incredible growth of faith, allowed us to see God's hand at work in our ministries, and had allowed us to see the incredible opportunity and power that the single stage of life carried for the Gospel. Yet, we found that pervasive negative attitudes abounded concerning the single stage of life. We watched as campus disciples avoided entering their singles ministries and spoke of how "dead" it was. We saw singles treating the single stage of life with the same outlook and enthusiasm as the DMV, and as such treated it with the same disinterest: pick a number and wait until you are finally sprung free from this dreadful place. This was the pervasive attitude that many singles witnessed. Marriage was therefore seen as salvation, and many treated the single stage of life as nothing more than a waiting period before your number was called, you got yourself the wife/husband God had in store for you, and then you could finally move on with your life. These attitudes have persisted in various forms and in varying degrees throughout various singles ministries in the majority of churches. The question for us was simple: Where do these attitudes come from? As we looked at Scripture and considered our own experiences, we knew there was a large disconnect between the attitudes that pervaded in this ministry, and the abundant opportunity God ascribes to singlehood in the Bible. Yet as we talked with single disciples around the country, we kept hearing the same story: singles ministries were struggling with disinterested membership, no real clarity of purpose, and a lack of meaningful investment from the bodies they were a part of. As we saw this pattern repeating in various singles ministries throughout the United States, and even hearing similar stories from singles in various countries overseas, it became clear that there was something off about how we were ministering to single Christians. Something that was not aligning them with God's Word and was not allowing us to see the full fruits of what the singles ministry could be.

Despite this, we have seen glimpses of what singles ministries can do when they are built on a proper foundation of Scripture, are given vision, and have the support of the larger bodies they are part of. We have seen these glimpses, and they are nothing short of powerful. This disconnect between the powerful glimpses we saw, and the pervading culture of pessimism within singles ministries was the soil in which this book project was planted.

This work was brought forth with the hope of exploring the reasons why a disconnect exists between what Scripture teaches about singlehood, and both the experience and condition of single Christians. It was also brought forth to provide a vision of what a singles ministry could be, and to share the very Scriptural foundations that support this vision. It was lastly brought forth to call the Church to action to look at their ministry to the single Christians and to single non-believers with fresh eyes, and to consider how they can invest in their singles, even if the investment is not financial.

The book contains pieces directed specifically at single disciples, as well as pieces directed to the body of Christ as a whole. You will see throughout this book, we all play a part in building up the body of Christ regardless of what stage of life we are in. As such, whether single or married, church leader or typical disciple, elder or newly baptized believer, you are encouraged to learn these lessons. You may find that God is calling you to this vision even if you are not single.

While the contents have been born out of the discussions and experiences of this group, it has been compiled by a single author. Where you see "I" statements made in this book, this is in reference to the author, Fernando Alejandro. You will also see "We" statements, which pertain to the experiences of the larger group. Therefore, in addition to the contributions of the author, this work also owes itself to the contributions, ideas, and experiences of Angela Perry, Angela Williams, Martin Ellis and Rosa Alejandro. You will hear more from them in chapter four, *Old-Fashioned Tent Revivals*.

Scope and Purpose of this Book

I wish to explain the scope of this book, acknowledge its limitations, and suggest how it might be used. While the experience of this small group has included meaningful interaction with single Christians from around the world, the most relevant experience we have is in an American church context. Although, this may very well speak to realities felt across the Western world and perhaps outside of a Western context as well, I do not pretend to know that as fact. As such, I wish to point out that the experiences described in this book are written from an American Christian context. We mention Christians outside of the United States having similar experiences as the ones outlined here, but I do not want to make sweeping statements about single Christians in contexts where we have fewer insights.

Additionally, even within an American context we acknowledge that experiences differ vastly from one church to another, so again, sweeping statements are not helpful. Therefore, the matters outlined in this book are describing real experiences, and real cultural influences, but are meant to be read and applied to your local church context. If you do not see any of the scenarios mentioned within this book as occurring in your church community, then amen. The Scriptural teachings laid out here can serve as an encouragement and reinforce what you already have built. However, I do believe the experiences communicated here will resonate deeply with single Christians and will be relevant to various church communities. I hope that you will take the lessons that apply to the conditions within your own specific church community, and those lessons that do not apply to you can remain as an encouragement to build upon what you have done.

Another acknowledgement concerning the scope of this book is that this is not a "how to" guide. This is not a step-by-step instruction on how to build a singles ministry. This is a launching pad. It is a vision, and a call to action. The step-by-step actions will need to be provided by you. There is not a one-size-fits-all approach to building a singles ministry or ministering to singles. We are inviting you and your local church family to work alongside God's Word to discover what those steps should be.

These admonitions should be used to call attention to a need and open a conversation. This book has sections devoted solely to single Christians, while other sections are meant to address church communities at large. The difficulty of addressing both single disciples and their larger church communities is that this book is not likely to be purchased by church communities, but by single Christians. As such, if you are a single Christian with this book in your hand, use this book to help start a conversation. It can be used to start a conversation within your singles ministry as well as with your evangelists, elders, and leaders. While the goal of the book is to bring attention to a need, it is done so in a spirit of love, unity, and truthfulness. We aim to maintain a spirit of brotherhood, peace, and kindness while also being forthright and to the point. I ask that the conversations that stem from this book have that same spirit of love, unity, and truthfulness.

Lastly, I wish to acknowledge that this book may touch upon matters where single Christians have felt hurt or neglected in the communities they worship with. I want to acknowledge that the anger or sadness felt in these instances are real, and I hope to God you find comfort, healing, and forgiveness. This book is a call to unity. This is not meant to cause division. It is not about "us vs them," which is where we can be tempted to go when we have been hurt. The only way forward is through unity. Division is the fruit of Satan, and we would be wise to identify it as such. We hope we can start the conversation and shed light on the single Christian experience in many churches. From here, the spirit of unity in Christ is certainly sufficient to bring us together to advance the work of God.

Terminology Used in this Book

Throughout these chapters, you will see Christian, and Disciple used interchangeably. This harkens back to Acts 11:26 where it states that the *"The disciples were called Christians first at Antioch."* The followers of Christ were, at an early stage labeled with the name "Christian," but it did not replace the fact that they saw themselves and referred to themselves as disciples. Where the word and practices of a "disciple" were understood in the ancient world, we may not fully grasp all its intricacies today. Therefore, I find it imperative that we aim to recover this word, and its fullness of meaning and practice, and how it should apply to us today. So, if you call yourself a Christian, then my assumption is that you are also a disciple of Christ, and vice versa. Thus, the terms appear interchangeably throughout this work.

Another feature of this work is the use of "life stage" in conjunction with the various ministry groupings common to American churches (Teen, Campus, Single, Married etc.). The term "life stage" is perhaps a dangerous one as it can convey that you are moving up stages of life. This is true perhaps of your teen and campus ministries, as one is defined by age, and the other is defined by educational pursuit. It only makes sense to move on from these ministries when you are no longer a teenager or have completed your educational goals. From this, many can take the term "life stages" to mean a progression from lower to higher, from teen to campus to singles to marrieds. But this is a false and unnecessary conclusion. Those who have gone through the challenges of losing a spouse or experiencing a divorce and find themselves single again, are not "moving down" in life stages. Nor are singles who get married "moving up." Your life stage is changing to be sure, but as this book will explore, this idea that you are moving up or down is not always applicable. Thus, "life stage" is not used in this book to connote progression, but rather to describe unique places of life where your needs and opportunities are distinct from other stages of life.

You may notice that the word "Church" is sometimes spelled with a capital letter, and other times left in lower case. This is done to differentiate between two common meanings of church. The capitalized spelling refers to the Church universal, that is the broader Church that exists for eternity and which all disciples of Christ across time are a part of. The lower-case spelling of church refers to your local church family. I find these distinctions helpful in order to differentiate between the specific congregations we worship in, and the broader Christian Church.

Speaking of ministry groupings used in American churches, it would be good to agree on terms. While the organization of American churches into various ministries based on life stages is common, the exact scope or titles given to these ministries can vary significantly. One churches "Youth Group" may be geared towards children up through college age, while others limit that group to high school students. Still others may go even beyond and include Christians up to age thirty or so. Having lived my experience in the International Churches of Christ, I am going to use the ministry designations that I have witnessed and participated in, which I will define here below. However, feel free to translate these terms to the various ministry groupings and names you use in your home congregations. For the sake of this book, I will be using the following terms and definitions:

Teen Ministry (or Youth Ministry): Comprised of teenagers up through their graduation from high school. The typical age range is from 13–18, though there are sometimes variations to this. Typically, the bulk of this ministry is comprised of the children of Christians who attend the church, though that is not always the case.

Campus Ministry: This is a ministry geared towards college students, typically in their undergraduate studies, though Masters/PhD students may participate in these groups as well. Though an age range is difficult to apply to this group, it is perhaps most common to see the bulk of members fall between the ages of 18–26.

Singles Ministry: This is a ministry comprised of unmarried Christians. Some are working full-time jobs, some are pursuing degrees, some may be retired, or some may not be working due to various life or health situations. The age range can fall anywhere between 18–100+, which is perhaps one of the challenges of organizing a group like this. The life experiences in this group range greatly from someone who is fresh out of school and starting their careers, to single parents, to widowed Christians, divorced Christians etc. It is quite varied, and the needs are therefore quite diverse.

Marrieds Ministry: This ministry is comprised of the married members of the Church. It can sometimes have subdivisions like young marrieds, or marrieds with children, and is typically focused on building strong marriage and family dynamics.

My description of these ministries, and in particular the singles ministry will vary from place to place. I am not proposing that these exact definitions be used for your own congregations. They are just the working definition being used for the sake of clarity. When I discuss singles ministry, I am speaking about two things. I am speaking about a formal organized ministry that is comprised of single Christians loosely described per the attributes stated earlier. I am also speaking of ministering to the single Christians in our churches who are loosely described per the attributes stated above. In other words, if you do not have a formal "singles ministry," you still have single Christians who fall under this category who your congregation ministers to. As such the vision in this book relates to both situations. Whether you have a singles ministry in your home church, or no formal ministry but have single brothers and sisters as part of the body you worship in, the scope of this book includes you.

While these ministries are set up to meet specific needs unique to the various life stages of our church members, it is worth noting that these ministries are not biblically defined groupings. We will not find mention of "singles" ministry, or "teen" ministry in the Bible. What we will find however are biblical teachings aimed at members in these various life stages. The intention of these ministries is to meet needs, and to provide a place to evangelize our peers within the communities we live in. We do not need to be overly dogmatic about these ministry descriptions. These definitions give us a starting point for this discussion, but are exactly that, a starting point.

Concluding Thoughts and Prayer

Our prayer is that this will help us to paint the singles ministry and the single stage of life in a biblical way, and for churches to support this vision for our singles. As such, we hope to eradicate the common attitudes and ideas that hinder our single brothers and sisters and replace these attitudes with the abundant Spirit-filled Words of God. However, you should not consider yourself to be a passive observer of this vision. In fact, you are being called to participate and build upon this vision.

Our prayer is that these thoughts can be a small spark to ignite the hearts of the saints towards action, but how this will impact your life and ministry is for God to reveal, and for you to be attentive to. We are excited that you are joining us in the exploration of this vision!

INTRODUCTION

Are Singles Coming to Church?

Culture is a powerful force. Through culture we understand and transmit our values, and we perpetuate our beliefs through the stories, activities, and practices we engage in. Culture often is not taught out right but is rather perceived and mimicked. It is both an organizing force, and a protective one. It allows us to communicate and understand one another and gives us a foundation to operate in our communities. Our culture is informed by both history and belief, along with so many other factors. Culture is a necessity in so far as we build one regardless of whether it is our intention to do so. There is much beauty and meaning in culture, and our engagement in cultural practices connects us with our forebears in ways these practices alone can achieve. But what happens when culture is built on a false premise? Or untrue suppositions are believed to be true, and are then encoded into the culture we build? The culture will continue to thrive and promulgate the untrue beliefs even though a tension between truth and culture will often be felt. As followers of Jesus Christ, we engage and are enriched by a larger Christian culture, under which we form many sub-cultures that are informed by our local histories and particular beliefs. This culture is a part of how we communicate our values, and there is some beauty to be experienced within it, but we must be aware that falsehoods can be encoded into our cultures, and we therefore act these falsehoods out without explicitly approving them. This of course is nothing new.

The history of Christianity is one of constant renewal, perpetuated by periods of practiced falsehoods which ranged from theological disagreements to outright evil, malicious, and dangerous actions perpetuated by those who claimed Christ as Lord. As far off as the Christian church has gotten throughout its history, it has always been called to judgement by the same source: God's Word. The Bible continuously teaches, corrects, rebukes, and trains us to be righteous (2 Timothy 3:16). Therein lies the beauty of our relationship to God. We can always look to the same source for guidance and understand our sins. We can always consider our culture in the context of what Scripture teaches. We can correct any errors that have arisen in our theological beliefs, or in our cultural practices, and honor God through our repentance and desire to elevate his Word in our communities. We can always peer into the mind of God, as he has chosen to reveal himself to us, and be transformed. It is for this reason that we must acknowledge that errors have and will seep into our lives and be perpetuated by our culture. And it is more so important that we understand our need to reflect on our practices and correct our culture when it does not align with the teachings of Christ (perhaps more now than ever).

It is here where I must turn my attention to the premise and focus of this book: the Christian attitude towards the single man and woman. It is in the Christian attitude towards our single men and women that I believe a rather egregious falsehood has seeped into our community of believers and has manifested unbiblical and harmful outcomes to our brothers and sisters as a result. To understand the error itself, I would like to first present the Scriptural truth that it undermines. We will discuss briefly what the Bible teaches, followed by a discussion on how the error manifests in our cultural practices, an explanation of the danger this poses to our evangelistic mission and testimony to the world, and lastly a proposed path forward that may elevate God's Word and move us in alignment with God's heart on the matter.

God's Plan for the Single Man and Woman

God created the covenant of marriage as a lasting commitment between three parties: the husband, the wife and God himself. Scripture elevates marriage in many ways. Proverbs 18:22 tells us that *"He who finds a wife finds a good thing and obtains favor from the LORD."* In Ephesians 5:25–33, Paul teaches that marriage is meant to be a living representation of Christ's love for the Church, and that both the love a husband has for his wife, and the respect the wife has for her husband, should mirror the relationship Christ has with the Church. This is no easy calling. Imagining the love Christ has for us, and the respect the Church is to have for Christ. Imagining the sacrifices, the serving and kind nature, the grace and mercy, the love made manifest in action, all the attributes that characterize the relationship between Christ and his Church and trying to live this out as a husband and a wife is a very high calling. I would pose that most of us who are married fall short of this calling if we even truly understand this to be the goal for our marriages.

Scripture elevates marriage in very distinct ways, and is something that has its origins in God, so we must never take the covenant of marriage lightly. It is important to understand that marriage has value, and the married man or woman have a high calling to honor God. As a married man myself, I can speak to the journey of love, sacrifice, and growth that the marriage covenant has brought into my life. I state all of this up front so that we can better understand the premise of what God's Word reveals in 1 Corinthians 7. I encourage you to read the entire chapter, but for the sake of this discussion, I will focus on verses 25–35:

1 Corinthians 7:25-35

[25]Now about virgins: I have no command from the Lord, but I give a judgment as one who by the Lord's mercy is trustworthy. [26]Because of the present crisis, I think that it is good for a man to remain as he is. [27]Are you pledged to a woman? Do not seek to be released. Are you free from such a commitment? Do not look for a wife. [28]But if you do

marry, you have not sinned; and if a virgin marries, she has not sinned. But those who marry will face many troubles in this life, and I want to spare you this.

[29]What I mean, brothers and sisters, is that the time is short. From now on those who have wives should live as if they do not; [30]those who mourn, as if they did not; those who are happy, as if they were not; those who buy something, as if it were not theirs to keep; [31]those who use the things of the world, as if not engrossed in them. For this world in its present form is passing away.

[32]I would like you to be free from concern. An unmarried man is concerned about the Lord's affairs—how he can please the Lord. [33]But a married man is concerned about the affairs of this world—how he can please his wife—[34]and his interests are divided. An unmarried woman or virgin is concerned about the Lord's affairs: Her aim is to be devoted to the Lord in both body and spirit. But a married woman is concerned about the affairs of this world—how she can please her husband. [35]I am saying this for your own good, not to restrict you, but that you may live in a right way in undivided devotion to the Lord.

This passage communicates a powerful identity to the single Christian. It is clear from the passage that Paul was relating this teaching within a context where crisis was occurring (v. 26). This context is important, as it can be difficult to square Paul's elevation of marriage in Ephesians 5, with his seeming dismissal of marriage here. The words in verses 26–31 are centered around maintaining one's current condition. In the face of this crisis, Paul was warning the believers regarding the challenges of pursuing a transition in their life. The Scripture does not specify what the crisis was but sets the premise by including its mention. From this point, Paul turns his attention to the distinction between married life and single life. He begins in verse 32 with the statement *"I would like you to be free from concern…"*. Paul goes on to describe how a married person has a necessary division of interests, but that a single person remains undivided in their devotion to the Lord. This division of interest for a married person is not wrong or sinful. The ministry of a married person includes their family, and this is an important function. It is through our ministry to our families that we can learn how to shepherd and care for our church family.

You can see the importance of this when Scripture includes the management of one's family as part of the eligibility for eldership (1 Timothy 3:1–5, Titus 1:6) and deaconship (1 Timothy 3:12). Yet the emphasis for Paul was not on marriage, but on the elevation of the single stage of life. A single man *"is concerned about the Lord's affairs—how he can please the Lord."* (v. 32). A single woman *"is concerned about the Lord's affairs: Her aim is to be devoted to the Lord in both body and spirit."* (v. 34). This teaching is not meant to restrict the single man or woman but rather for them to *"live in a right way in undivided devotion to the Lord."* (v. 35). Through Paul, the Holy Spirit communicated an identity to leave behind for those of us in the single stage of life. Here God communicates an identity that is defined by its devotion to the Lord. This devotion is one that incorporates both body and spirit and maintains a focus on pleasing God rather than pleasing a relationship. There is an incredible opportunity that is being presented in this statement. It means that for the single individual, for as long as their single stage of life lasts, there is an opportunity to devote it to God and his kingdom entirely. This opportunity closes in marriage, as the person's life begins to be focused on the ministry of family. It cannot be emphasized enough that the opportunity provided in singlehood is one that can bring much glory to the kingdom of God and can be used to communicate the Gospel in a world that so sorely needs it.

Paul exemplified this. As a single man, he made sacrifices for the Gospel, going where he was needed, and preaching the good news about Jesus throughout the Roman world. His calling to preach to the Gentiles was one he took as his primary purpose, and he saw that despite the beauty and divine purposes behind marriage, it was the unmarried stage of life that was optimal for these purposes. I emphasize again that this is not to downplay marriage, or to state that a married person cannot make sacrifices for the sake of the Gospel. It is simply that the married person must make sacrifices only after they have accounted for their primary responsibility to their families. Mark 1:30 makes mention of Simon Peter's mother-in-law, so we know that he was a married man who made great sacrifices for the kingdom. It is possible that other apostles were married men as well. Yet it is interesting to note that Jesus never married, and Paul, the apostle responsible for nearly two thirds of our New Testament was unmarried. It is also clear that Timothy who led one of the largest churches in the first-century was single. In short, single people can use the opportunity accorded by their relationship status to accomplish great things for God.

Why does this matter? It matters for two important reasons. First, it shows that the calling for the unmarried disciple is actually a lofty one. Scripture presents an identity for unmarried disciples that is wrapped up in their capacity to focus on the affairs of God. It is striking how much the ancient world and early Christians honored the man or woman who devoted themselves to God entirely and took an oath of celibacy to maintain that focus for life. In later years, the Catholic church made this a requirement for the priesthood, but it had its precedence in this passage from 1 Corinthians 7. In the ancient Church, the unmarried man or woman was recognized as being able to minister in a capacity that a married man or woman could not. The unmarried man or woman who devoted themselves to God was honored and respected in these early Christian communities. This was the fruit of passages like 1 Corinthians 7:25–35, and certainly the example of Paul that gave the early Christians (and indeed us today) a worthwhile representation of what that fruit looks like.

So then where have we gone wrong? Have we failed to honor this passage? Do we not teach this passage in the modern Church, or often apply it incorrectly?

Recognized by its Fruit

It is not a question as to whether we incorrectly teach this passage. I believe that many churches that teach the Bible honor the heart of this passage and encourage their singles with its meaning. So, what is the problem? The problem is not how we teach this passage specifically. It is what our cultural practices teach our singles that becomes problematic. We may teach that the unmarried stage of life is blessed, but do our practices reflect this honor and elevation of singlehood? Or do our practices instead inadvertently devalue the single stage of life? The following are a few examples of how culture has altered our practices toward, and treatment of, single Christians in many churches.

Is Marriage or Righteousness the Goal?

As a Church, it is right that we teach marriage as having the meaning, value, and dignity that God has given to it. As such, it is right to elevate marriage. Yet we must be clear that marriage is not a "better" stage than being single. It is a special covenant to be sure, a blessing from God. But so is singlehood, and Scripture is clear of the blessed state of the single disciple. Free of the concerns of this world, undivided devotion to God, concerned for the affairs of the Divine. These are the descriptions that God gives the single stage of life through his Scripture. As such, the message our single men and women should hear consistently is one of opportunity and devotion. Yet the most consistent message our single disciples receive is that they should be married. That something is wrong if they are not married. For the most part, this is not stated directly from the pulpit. This instead comes out in the ways that we treat our unmarried brothers and sisters within our fellowships. How our church culture treats singles.

A personal example may be of use here. As a single man, I was leading a singles ministry in my local congregation, leading a teachers group responsible with developing midweek lessons for the church, engaging in evangelism, and seeing God produce fruit throughout all these ministry endeavors. It was an enriching time for me spiritually. Yet when I was approached in fellowship, I did not receive questions about ministry, or teaching, or evangelism. Instead, I was consistently asked about my dating life. "Why are you still single?" was the most common question I was asked. Now, I believe my brothers and sisters were good in their intentions. But the pervasive attitude behind this question and the conversations that followed them was something to the effect of "You are too spiritual to be single." This came from an unspoken belief that marriage was the progression of maturity and spirituality. We have seen very few examples in modern times of single men and women becoming evangelists in our churches. The leaders are typically raised up from amongst the married brothers and sisters. So, it is easy to conflate the spiritual maturity required for leadership and the fact that our leaders are uniformly married to mean that to be married must mean that you are spiritually mature. This is where our culture has betrayed the truth of Scripture.

Even though we may teach 1 Corinthians 7 as being true, our church life does not reflect this truth. Scripture spoke of my singleness being an asset, yet my church culture was communicating that my efforts in ministry were secondary to, and less relevant than my marital status. Now if this were just my own isolated experience, it would not be cause for concern. Yet when I speak with single disciples from around the world, I have heard the same consistent story being told. Culture perpetuates over time, and I fear that we have not only been infiltrated by an untruth, but that this practice has been woven into our culture across geographic boundaries, and across time. We must question whether we are building a ministry whose primary focus is pleasing the Lord, or whose primary focus is getting married.

The correct application will be a ministry that will grow and flourish. The latter ministry will typically shrink and discourage the singles. The reason is that if marriage is the only goal, then some will get married, some will leave the Church to pursue marriage, and others will not get married, and remain in a group whose primary focus of marriage is something they do not seek to do. So, they check out. This is not a strategy for success. Is there still a place in the Christian church for the celibate man or woman that is not on the periphery? A place that honors their contributions and elevates their service to the church? In the early church it was. What are we communicating to the single men and women in our churches? Are we communicating a vision that is limited to just marriage? Or are we communicating the incredible opportunity for righteousness and devotion to God that they can have? It is important to note that these are not mutually exclusive pursuits. One can devote themselves to God and be open to building towards marriage. However, we must ask ourselves whether we promote one to the detriment of the other. If all the church has to offer singles is marriage, then we have already failed. We cannot operate as if marriage is the ultimate goal of the single Christian man or woman. A relationship with God, eternity, salvation, meaning, purpose, grace these are just a few qualities that the Gospel of Christ offers us. This is what singlehood should be focused on. Certainly, we can help those who wish to marry to pursue godly dating relationships, but this should be a secondary feature of a singles ministry. Righteousness, and undivided devotion to the affairs of the Lord should be primary.

Placing Limits

In addition to the message that marriage should be the primary focus for singles, there can often be limitations placed on unmarried disciples in Christian community. There are a number of exceptional single disciples, men and women who are leaders in their respective industries, business leaders, thought leaders, who are well respected, and well regarded in the companies and networks they navigate. Additionally, they desire to serve the church with the gifts they have. But they often find limits to how much they are allowed to do within the church. There is a Biblical injunction to base the criteria about eldership and deaconship on marriage, yet leadership is depicted as a spiritual gift, which can be manifested by any member of the body of Christ (Romans 12:8). To what extent do we allow the unmarried disciple in our fellowship to serve in leadership roles? Often, our single disciples are sent to serve with our youth, or with our college students, and these are worthy ministries to be sure. But what about single disciples teaching and leading married men and women? Is there concern about having singles lead marrieds in different capacities? Are singles represented on our leadership teams? On our boards? Are they represented on our staffs? If the singles in your church make up a significant portion of your population and their voice is absent from your leadership teams, how well can their spiritual needs and opportunities be communicated or met? These are all worthwhile questions to ask to evaluate the position of our singles within our churches.

I must be clear; I am not saying that the mere state of singlehood qualifies the single disciple to lead or teach or preach. Only the example of their life, their devotion to the affairs of the Lord, and the presence of God's Holy Spirit bearing fruit in their ministry can show who is ready to lead or teach or preach. Yet a consistent theme we have gathered from speaking to single Christians is this sense that barriers and ceilings can be placed on their contributions, particularly in areas of leadership. Consider that if we only hire "ministry couples" to lead our various ministries, then singles are by definition already excluded from contributing in these roles, regardless of their giftedness and experience to do so.

Again, these are not things we teach from the pulpit, but they are often encoded in our ministries. This is not a battle of married vs. unmarried disciples, but rather a question of how we elevate the gifts and contributions of each individual disciple of Christ, and whether we limit those contributions for reasons that do not find their root in God's Word. Do our singles have avenues to use the various gifts within our communities? For those gifted in leadership, are we using them in leadership roles and allowing those gifts to flourish in our midst?

The Investment into Our Single Disciples

If you want to consider the priorities of any entity, it is often as easy as looking at where they make the most investments. It is often the case that churches invest heavily into their teen and campus ministries, and there are good practical reasons for this. Many parents do not want to be in a church where their children are not being engaged spiritually and campus ministries have typically been the place of greatest numerical growth for many church ministries. This strategy has proven quite fruitful over time. Consider also that providing staff for a teen or campus setting is a much smaller financial obligation. You can hire young ministers to lead in teen or campus ministry settings, and the cost of hiring younger staff with less experience is far more manageable than hiring a more seasoned staff that would be required for a mature singles ministry. The investments in teen and campus ministries are good and valuable investments to make. Yet I wonder if churches have considered making the extra sacrifice to invest in their single disciples. It is rare that singles ministries have paid staff who are devoted exclusively to building their ministries, even if single disciples make up a significant portion of the congregation. The message is often that there is not enough money to go around, and if money becomes available, it can then be used for the singles ministry. Yet when money becomes available it often gets funneled directly back to the various ministries that already receive investment. This shows that the issue is not one of finances, but of priorities. If we do not believe that we devalue our single brothers and sisters theologically or in placing limitations to their service within our churches, we may find that we devalue them financially. The result is that our single brothers and sisters can often feel neglected or like their ministry is not a priority for the churches they worship in.

Campus Disciples Fear/Avoid the Singles Ministry

There is a common reputation the singles stage of life has in many of our college fellowships. The reputation is that the singles ministry is essentially a "dead" ministry. There is not much in the way of evangelism and baptisms, and we often hear from campus students that their singles ministries do not inspire them. The singles ministry events are few and far between (which can be quite jarring for those coming out of a campus ministry environment that is event heavy), and in essence, singles ministry feels like a holding cell where one awaits the day they are blessed enough to be married and leave. As such, marrying out of college is the best-case scenario, and the second best-case scenario is to avoid the singles any way you can: stay in the campus, volunteer for the teens, anything that will allow you to skip the singles ministry altogether. What surprises me about these depictions, is that they are the exact same descriptions I heard when I was a college student twenty years ago. This reputation has remained unchanged over time. If this is how our young men and women speak about the single stage of life, or of the singles ministries in their churches, then it is quite clear that they are entering into what should be one of the most spiritually invigorating opportunities of their life with fear, and avoidance.

All change is scary, and the transition from college to working life is no different, but I fear that we have built a culture where college students are happy to become married working Christians, but fear becoming single working Christians. What is the attitude of your college students regarding the single stage of life? Have we failed to communicate the vision of 1 Corinthians 7 to our young brothers and sisters? If they are ready to be married and not ready to be single, there is something wrong in the way we are preparing them.

If none of this sounds like your fellowship, then amen! If you are not single, it would be worthwhile to ask your single brothers and sisters whether they feel that any of the items listed above are true. This really is about love for our family. There will be those of us who read through these items and acknowledge that some of these descriptions are spot on. Amen for this too. It is first necessary to see where we stand so that we can determine where we must go. There will be more about this further along. Whether you find that your congregation strongly supports its unmarried brethren, or not, I ask you to consider the question below.

Are We Raising Up Paul's in Our Churches?

This question is what haunts me regarding our single brothers and sisters. If we are a community that honors the truth of 1 Corinthians 7:25–35, then we should see the fruit of this present in our churches. Men and women devoted to the mission, preaching the Gospel around the world. By its fruits, we will recognize our teaching, will we not? So what fruit are we producing? Are we raising up single men and women prepared to devote their single stage of life to spreading the Gospel? And if so, do we see this just in the singles who are fresh out of college? Or do we see singles in their 30s, 40s, 50s and beyond inspired to devote their singleness to the affairs of the Lord?

This is where we are losing a great opportunity. When our single brothers and sisters do not find an outlet to serve within the fellowship, they often concentrate their talents in their careers or other interests. I believe this to be a big loss for the church, and it is a loss perpetuated by church culture. But with this loss comes a tremendous opportunity. Imagine realizing that a quarter or a third of your body was being underutilized, and that if you simply changed a few habits, you would see the full benefits and potential of what a healthy body can do? I believe this to be the opportunity we see right now. By rooting out cultural influences that do not align with Scripture, we could see a significant portion of our church bodies come to life. Consider the implications of that for our service in the community, our evangelism, in all our work in the Lord.

There is also one last matter to consider that is by no means the least of our considerations. This is something that every disciple, whether married or unmarried must be concerned with. While we have discussed the danger of this cultural influence on the spiritual condition of our single brothers and sisters, we must also consider the danger this poses to our testimony and mission in this world.

Are Singles Coming to Church?

How are we doing in our evangelism of single men and women in our communities? And when we have brought them to a knowledge of Christ, do they thrive in our congregations? These are serious questions that should be taken into consideration. The single population is an ever growing one, and this population is varied in its experiences. According to the Pew Research Center, in 2019 approximately 38%

1. See "Rising Share of U.S. Adults Are Living Without a Spouse or Partner" by Richard Fry and Kim Parker. Source: https://www.pewresearch.org/social-trends/2021/10/05/rising-share-of-u-s-adults-are-living-without-a-spouse-or-partner/

of adults ages 25-54 are unpartnered (meaning neither married nor living with a partner).[1] This is up sharply from the 29% that it was in 1990 (see the article in the footnotes for more details). Marriage within the larger American context is in decline, and when people are getting married, it is at older ages than ever before.[2] In other words, the single population is growing sharply, and our singles ministries are our evangelistic arms to reach this population. Are we prepared for this? Do we have ministries where singles, of all ages and experiences can escape the world and thrive spiritually? Are we prepared to present the Gospel within this context, and provide the spiritual resources that single men and women need from their spiritual families?

There is a real opportunity to communicate Christ to a group of people who could then become exemplars of 1 Corinthians 7:25–35. Men and women who can devote more time to the affairs of God for as long as they remain single. This should be seen as an incredible opportunity. Not only do we have an opportunity to communicate Christ, but for the single disciple who chooses marriage, we have the chance to help them build their relationships on the foundation of God's Word. And for those who choose to remain unmarried, we have the chance to communicate the identity provided to them by God, as men and women living in undivided devotion to the Lord. Both states have dignity, meaning and

2. Median age of marriage has risen from 26.1 (for men) and 23.9 (for women) in 1990 to 30.4 (for men) and 28.6 (for women) in 2021. See Census Bureau "Table MS-2. Estimated Median Age at First Marriage, by Sex: 1890 to the Present". Source: https://www.census.gov/data/tables/time-series/demo/families/marital.html

value, and it is our responsibility to communicate that to a world that is increasingly skeptical and cynical of marriage.

The world needs our testimony, and the better we can equip ourselves to carry the Gospel to the populations who live in our midst, the more effective we are for God. Let us not allow an error of culture to derail our testimony in this world. Let us not allow fallacies to limit what God can produce within the lives of our single brothers and sisters. Let us bring into alignment the word we preach from the pulpit with the actual beliefs and practices that we hold.

What is the Fruit we are Producing?

I conclude by asking you to consider the following question: what is the fruit you are seeing in your singles ministries? Do you see paragons of undivided devotion to the Lord? Or do you see a group exemplified more by aloofness, self-focus, and lack of spiritual vision? If your singles exemplify the former, then I believe you are seeing the fruit of right doctrine, and proper inspiration. However, if your singles exemplify the latter, then I call you to consider that perhaps it is showing the fruit of your culture. As is true of the church, when one part of the body suffers, the whole part suffers (1 Corinthians 12:26). This is a ministry concern, not just the concern of our single brothers and sisters. We as a Church have a duty to build up the body of Christ, to represent God's Word properly, to elevate truth, and make sure that our identity is defined by God. We cannot allow ourselves to be blind to these concerns, and we cannot allow ourselves to miss the latent opportunity that lies before us. This is not an indictment, but an encouragement. We have a chance to elevate God's Word properly and build up our fellowship. We have a chance to spur growth and maturity, where we have not always seen it before. We have a chance to powerfully proclaim the Gospel message to an ever-growing segment of the population. But our approach must change. We must stop thinking of this ministry as a dead zone, or as a holding period for marriage. We must start communicating a greater vision of what this stage of life can be, one that is tied to God's Word and heart for our single brothers and sisters.

Do We See Through a Lens of Scripture or Culture?

One of the challenges I see is a refusal to look at the term "single" from the perspective provided from Scripture. "Do we have to call ourselves the 'singles ministry'?" Was a common question I heard. "We're the only ministry that's defined by what we don't have." This statement alone reflects the acceptance of a lie. The recent trend to rebrand "singles ministry" to Yo Pro (young professionals), or Professionals ministry, I believe is misguided. Out of disdain for the term "Single," we instead orient our identity around our jobs. This is done to frame our ministries in terms of what we have, instead of what we do not have, but I think that this way of thinking is built on a false premise. If we look at our lives as single disciples and conclude that our collective identity should be centered around our jobs, then we are not looking at this through the lens of Scripture. Why abandon everything that 1 Corinthians 7:25–35 tells us we gain from singlehood? What lens are we using to gauge these questions? If we have not scripturally grounded our identities, then what are they grounded in? It is certainly not wrong to rebrand or rename our groups, but we must question whether our motivations are rooted in an incorrect belief.

The error is in the initial supposition that in being called "single" we are being defined by what we lack. Scripture is clear that we do not lack, but rather we gain. We gain something special and unique that may only last for a short time. We gain an undivided devotion to the Lord, a concern for the affairs of the Lord, we gain a power and crown that if submitted to God will see the power of the Gospel raise up in our very midst: salvation brought to our communities, the poor elevated through our service, a Church enriched by our contributions, the gospel proclaimed around the world. If this is what this singles identity grants us, why would we abandon that for something as simple as our professions? It is fine to rename your ministries and forge an identity, just ensure that you have rooted this identity in biblical truth

The Blame Game Lands on Satan

For singles who may feel hurt or even resentful because they have felt disregarded, ignored, or stifled within their congregations, I wish to encourage you with the following words. It can be very tempting to look for someone to blame. However, if we are to assign blame, we must identify the proper culprit. The spirit of lies and falsehood draws a direct line to Satan. As Jesus tells us about Satan: *"When he lies, he speaks his native language, for he is a liar and the father of lies."* (John 8:44). It is wrong for disciples to consider this as a matter of "us" versus "them." Singles versus marrieds. We are together the body of Christ. We must not allow divisions of this kind to occur as they are manifestations of Satan himself. I believe that our churches and our church leaders are doing their best to proclaim the Gospel and help others know Christ. This is where we can stand alongside our leaders and offer to hold up their arms as Aaron and Hur did for Moses (Exodus 17:10-13). That a congregation has short-comings, or has outright sin is a static truth that will remain a reality until the day we all reach Heaven. Even a passing glance at the letters of Paul to the various churches will reveal as much. This is where we must exercise grace and look to work together to advance the cause of Christ.

The single disciple must take ownership of themselves, their beliefs, and their God-defined identity. This ministry cannot only look to the rest of the congregation to give them their identity, their worth, their mission. God gave that to you. Now own it. Once you are invested in your own ministry, you will see how much God can do with you.

The Challenge of Ministry

We have explored several ways that our culture can undermine our single disciples, and the danger this poses to our mission. I now want to turn our attention to how we can build up our singles ministries. I wish to present a new vision for our single brothers and sisters. A new vision for how we pursue ministering to this stage of life, and how we can build up our singles within our fellowship. A vision for how we can communicate the heart of God and inspire the next Paul's in our communities. This vision begins first with a direct message to our single brothers and sisters. Despite what may be practiced or taught, whether directly or indirectly, in the congregation you attend regarding the single stage of life, the vision begins with you. It begins with the responsibility you must take, and the identity you must claim. It begins with your understanding of what the single stage of life is. It begins with understanding the powers and crowns you hold.

I think it is important to also note that singles also can't do everything and be glorified babysisters. They also must pay careful attention to their work and being model employees or students. This is also a time for them to hone their skills, increase their knowledge and advance their career. The important difference is that they are in a unique period of life where their relationship loyalties are undivided. As a result they have opportunities for great impact in advancing the kingdom of God.

CHAPTER ONE

Of Powers and Crowns

It was a simple idea that sparked the movement. A movement that grew and overthrew its immediate boundaries. It disrupted empires, and overthrew political, social, and economic systems. It has been abused, altered, manipulated because the power it held was too tempting for the corrupt and the ignorant. Yet at its core lay a simple principle. Simple does not necessarily mean easy, but graspable, attainable. It means that anyone can have it. It is incredible to think of the countless number of saints who have lived under its rule, and the stories and ambitions that it fueled have changed the course of human history as we know it. But all good things come under attack, and this is doubly true for the greater things. The kingdom of God is beyond a great thing, and it has enemies. Enemies who understand its power and fear it, and who will do anything to stop it. And yet the kingdom of God used this simple idea as a manifestation of God to us. This idea is simple, and it is called grace. Grace started a movement that altered the world, has been corrupted, come under attack, and yet persists to this day as a beacon of hope drawing us to the eternal. The very starting point of our discussion is *Of Powers and Crowns.*

The apostle Paul tells us in 1 Corinthians 15:10:

"¹⁰But by the grace of God I am what I am, and his grace to me was not without effect. No, I worked harder than all of them—yet not I, but the grace of God that was with me."

For Paul, this grace produced within him an outlook that would fuel his desire for God's kingdom. Not by his own strength, but by the strength that God's grace had provided him. Many consider Paul to be a prime example of what an unmarried disciple can do. From his one encounter with the incarnate Christ, Paul (through God's grace) became the catalyst that brought the Gospel to the Western World. Whole nations of people were introduced to the Gospel, souls were saved, letters of instructions provided for generations to come, and an example of life have all been left behind by a man who had a single encounter with Christ.

To be single and a disciple of Christ has been misunderstood. In the previous section, we outlined ways that our church culture can fall short in communicating the value of singlehood. Yet those are not the only ways culture has communicated erroneous ideas. Sometimes, single disciples themselves believe false ideas concerning their singlehood. I have heard singlehood interpreted as a moral failure, a punishment from God for errors of the past, or any number of interpretations that understand singlehood as punitive. Marriage conversely has been interpreted as a release from the prison of singlehood, and a sign that God has now forgiven whatever transgressions that led to that imprisonment. In this way, singlehood is only viewed in its relation to marriage. But what if we considered singlehood in its relation to Christ? Or to the kingdom of God? Is it possible our perception towards this state of life has become altered, corrupted as the enemy knows how to do so well?

Within the larger Christian world at present, the single state of life has not been given the attention it deserves. A brief perusal through the Christian literature shows many titles dedicated towards preparing for marriage, finding your perfect match, staying pure, all of which define singlehood only in its relation to marriage. These are worthwhile topics to be sure, but only a few titles are dedicated towards the question of how singles can use this stage of life to build the kingdom of God. I consider this an error. The single state of life is often lived with one purpose in mind: getting married. This book posits another perspective: that the single state of life is an opportunity like no other to impact the world for Christ. To this end, I turn to one of the themes of this book: Of Powers and Crowns. There is rich meaning behind this term that will be explored below. It fixes our attention on the tools and assets we have been given to glorify God. It represents what the undivided devotion to God, that 1 Corinthians 7:35 speaks of, can look like. The idea of powers and crowns comes from an awe-inspiring scene shown in Revelation 4:4, 9–11:

> 4Surrounding the throne were twenty-four other thrones, and seated on them were twenty-four elders. They were dressed in white and had crowns of gold on their heads.
>
> 9Whenever the living creatures give glory, honor and thanks to him who sits on the throne and who lives for ever and ever, 10the twenty-four elders fall down before him who sits on the throne and worship him who lives for ever and ever. They lay their crowns before the throne and say:
>
> 11"You are worthy, our Lord and God,
>   to receive glory and honor and power,
> for you created all things,
>   and by your will they were created
> and have their being."

This is a scene of worship, where God Almighty appears at the center of this heavenly stage, and surrounding him are twenty-four elders, each of which have been dressed in white with a crown of gold sitting on their heads. A crown is a symbol of rule, power, and authority. Kings and queens wear crowns, and it signals their sovereignty over their kingdom. It is fascinating to think that these twenty-four elders represented individuals who had rule, power, and authority.

They sat surrounding the throne of God, a position of honor and prestige, and they sat upon thrones, another symbol of power, rule, and authority. These were powerful people, appearing as part of the heavenly host, favored by God to be able to sit in his presence. Yet the scene continues with a description of their worship. As God is being praised, and glory, honor and thanks are given to him, it tells us that the elders fall down. An undignified act for someone in a position of power to do. They separated themselves from the seat of power they held and took a position of obeisance, of humility. Yet their next action puts this previous one in perspective. It tells us that *"They lay their crowns before the throne."* They removed the very symbol of power, rule, and authority over their kingdoms from their heads and cast it before God as God was being praised. It is a scene that conveys an idea that the great power, rule, and authority that man has is worthless before the throne of God. Our thrones are worth abandoning, and our crowns worth discarding when we sit before the one and only true power that is God.

The passage does not end there. It goes on to tell us what these twenty-four elders say after casting their crowns before God. They say: *"You are worthy, our Lord and God, to receive glory and honor and power."* To honor God and give glory to God are things that we commonly hear in the context of our worship. We see these concepts recorded throughout Scripture. Yet it is that last part that we will set our focus upon: giving "power" to God. What does this mean? God is all powerful, so what would it mean for God to receive power? The fact of the matter is that God is indeed all powerful. There is nothing he needs from us. Yet the passage does not tell us that God needs power, but that God is worthy to receive power. So then what is this power this passage is referring to?

The very acts of worship and humility the elders are demonstrating perhaps provide some insight into this. For when they climb down off their thrones, a symbol of their position, and cast off their crowns, a symbol of authority, what are they doing if not submitting their power to God? This submission is not simply them giving up their power, but rather acknowledging that God is greater, and their power is worthless before this God. That the most valuable items or positions they have are considered nothing, and they would readily, and easily submit the power they have to give glory to the King of Kings. This very act is tied to the realization presented in verse 11 where it reads *"for you created all things, and by your will they were created and have their being."* When we understand that we stand before the Creator of the Universe, we can then begin to evaluate the true worth of things. The things we cherish most may appear worthless once we understand this. And the things we devoted our entire lives to build, may well be the very things we cast away so easily when we truly understand this.

Now this may be nice as a theological reflection, but how does this apply to our lives? The truth is that we as Christians carry many authorities, and powers that we can and should submit to God. The jobs we work, the money we earn, the networks we navigate, the skills and knowledge we own are all powers we have, whether they are small or great. We can submit these small thrones or crowns to God by using them for his kingdom. When we conduct ourselves in our jobs in ways that promote high ethics, and excellence before God, and use the opportunities provided for us to elevate God in our workplace, then we are using our job not just for our own purposes, but for God's purposes. When we take the money we earn, and use it to promote the Gospel, whether by investing in church plantings, in service to the poor, or any of the other numerous ways accorded to us, then we are submitting the power of money to effectuate the kingdom of God on this earth. When we use our networks to bring people together to work for the purposes of the kingdom, we are using this power for God. And when we take the skills and knowledge we own and use them to build new ministries and initiatives to help further the teachings and ministry of the kingdom of God, we have effectively submitted this power to be used for God's purposes.

All of these "powers" outlined above should be relevant to any disciple regardless of marital or life status. We all have something, whether small or great that we can submit to God. We may think that in becoming a disciple that we have submitted everything to God, but it does not take much thought to see that this is not always true. We can call Jesus Lord, and still be hesitant to use our money for his kingdom or stand up for morality and truth in our workplace, or neglect proclaiming the very Gospel that brought us to God in the first place. Yet it is our calling to do so. To pick up our crosses daily and follow Christ (Luke 9:23). Although this concept of submitting our powers and crowns is true for all disciples, there is one way that this idea of submitting our powers and crowns to God relates specifically to single disciples, and not to the married disciples. Your singleness itself is a unique and valuable power that only you can submit to God. The single stage of life carries with it certain attributes, challenges, and opportunities that if used for the purposes of God's kingdom can produce an abundance of fruit for you and the church body you are a part of. Your singleness is a powerful force, the weight of which can move your communities in service, in missions, in evangelism, in generosity, in all the ways that God has gifted you to impact this world.

Singleness as a Power for God's Kingdom

The single stage of life offers a unique opportunity in the ways that Paul described in 1 Corinthians 7:25–35, which were covered in the introduction of this book. Here we will focus in on the specific verses between v.32–35:

> [32]I would like you to be free from concern. An unmarried man is concerned about the Lord's affairs—how he can please the Lord. [33]But a married man is concerned about the affairs of this world—how he can please his wife—[34]and his interests are divided. An unmarried woman or

virgin is concerned about the Lord's affairs: Her aim is to be devoted to the Lord in both body and spirit. But a married woman is concerned about the affairs of this world—how she can please her husband. [35]I am saying this for your own good, not to restrict you, but that you may live in a right way in undivided devotion to the Lord.

Paul identifies a few specific characteristics of the single life that he believes provide a unique opportunity. The verse starts off with Paul saying that he wants the listeners to be free from concern. He then goes on to tie a married persons concerns to their spouses and thus needing to be concerned about the affairs of this world. Typically, when the term "world" is used, it is referring to something sinful and ungodly, though I do not believe that to be its meaning here (Ephesians 5:25–33 helps dispel this notion). So, I believe this to be a more technical description. When you are married you fill yourself with concern over earthly matters: where will we live? What school will our kids go to? Why is my spouse mad at me? How do we work out this problem with the dishes? And so forth. If anyone has spent time around newly married couples, it does not take long to find that an exorbitant amount of time is spent working out issues that are largely trivial in the large scheme of things. I believe that even that has a purpose, because as a married couple, the trivial things are helping build their oneness, and each problem that is resolved is a manifestation of the unity of Christ. But if we are comparing two hours spent being counseled over an argument on whether the toothpaste cap should stay on or off, and two hours spent in a Bible study helping someone to know Christ, then I think we can understand why the concerns over the affairs of the world might be viewed as trivial.

Now I must be clear, it is obvious that a married person can be in Bible studies helping others know Christ and engage and all forms of ministry. That is not the point of this example. The point is that the married couple will necessarily have to devote time to matters that the single disciple does not need to bother themselves with. So it could be that when this hypothetical married couple were two single individuals, they found themselves free and able to take on various ministry roles and serve in many ways. Now that they are married, they may find that they cannot engage in ministry to the extent that they could before. This is not wrong, evil, or sinful, it is simply a part of the married stage of life.

Or consider the example of going on a church planting, or on a one-year challenge, or overseas on the mission field. These decisions require great sacrifice regardless of what stage of life you are in. Yet compare trying to make this decision as a married person (as many have), compared to an unmarried person (as many also have). There will be more that the married person must consider, and perhaps more to sacrifice that the single disciple does not need to concern themselves with, even though they are considering the same calling. There have been incredible examples of sacrifice from both married and unmarried individuals when it comes to the mission, but Paul's description here is a summation of these two stages of life, and who has more "concerns" to consider. His conclusion was that the married person had more to be concerned with, while the unmarried person could remain concerned simply with the affairs of the Lord. Just consider the ways that Paul describes the unmarried stage of life in these verses:

1) Concerned with the affairs of the Lord. (v. 32)
2) Concerned with how one can please the Lord. (v. 32)
3) Devoted to the Lord in body and in spirit. (v. 34)
4) Undivided devotion to the Lord. (v. 35)

Paul sees an opportunity for unmarried people that he believes is simply not available to someone who is married. The question is whether you believe this to be true. You must understand that this opportunity is only present for as long as you are single. The opportunity closes at marriage. Do you believe that you can use this stage of life for God's incredible purposes? Do you see what you can build for God and his kingdom in this stage of life? Or conversely, are you wasting this stage of life? Are you simply waiting for a spouse? Are you believing the lies that this stage of life is like purgatory, and you are simply bidding your time awaiting your release? Do you understand the power you have in your singlehood, and what you could become if you would simply lay your crown at God's feet?

The Question of Time

It is often believed that the greatest asset a single disciple has is their time. I do not think this is necessarily true. From what Paul is describing, I believe that the greatest asset a single disciple has is their autonomy. The amount of time a single disciple has varies from person to person and is largely dependent on stage of life and particular life situation. Being single does not neatly fit into one category after all, there are various experiences within singlehood, and each state has its own opportunities and challenges. The single parent has a very different command on their time than a single person without children. Just as the single person who cares for an ailing family member (as becomes a more common experience for older singles) has less time than a single person who does not have this responsibility. What is more is that the single disciple must handle their responsibilities entirely. Where a married couple can divide responsibilities between the husband and wife, the single individual must handle all responsibilities for themselves. So, where a married couple can send the husband to pick up dinner while the wife runs errands at the post office, the single person will often be doing both. This is of course a generalization, and this varies greatly person to person, but generally, I have found that the assumption of free time for singles may not be as true a supposition as sometimes believed. Where the allowance of free time may have its restrictions, the autonomy that a single has is truly where their power lies. Ask yourself this question, after all your responsibilities are done for the week, how much time do you have left? Whether that number is 1 hour or 100 hours, the truth is that as a single disciple, you have a level of autonomy over that time that is not held in other stages of life. A married person takes the free time available to them and devotes some to their spouse, some to their children, and then whatever is left can be negotiated with the spouse. A single person can jump straight to a final estimation: using their time as they please. This is the opportunity that the single has.

This talk of free time, and how it can be used, may bring up mixed feelings. For some singles, the desire to be in a relationship, makes the talk of free time a bitter pill to swallow. Free time is often a reminder of their desire for a romantic relationship, and can often conjure feelings of loneliness, sadness, and longing. I know this struggle, and I do not discount these feelings. I do not believe there to be a magic formula to finding the right mate if that is your desire (though there is no shortage of books on this topic for you to choose from!). I spent many years spiritually aloof, longing for a relationship and hoping to find the "right one." I recall at points feeling bitter, or simply discouraged over the seeming lack of traction in this arena of my life. I truthfully believed my singleness to be a failure (lies from the enemy), and I despised this stage of life. I had a choice at this point in my life. I could either live out my single years in a constant pity party, or I can engage in the ministry I knew God wanted me to be engaged in. So, I committed to serve in God's kingdom. I evangelized, I studied the Bible with people, I served and shepherded younger disciples, I said "yes" to the needs that arose from the body of believers. I said "yes" to helping people move, "yes" to serving in kids kingdom, "yes" to song leading (that probably should have been a "no"). In time, I was asked to lead the singles ministry, and I said "yes" to that too. I was asked about organizing a teacher's group, and I said "yes" to that. All the while, I went on dates with my incredible sisters in Christ, I took advantage of opportunities to fellowship and build great friendships with other singles, I had great experiences, served with *HOPE Worldwide* in different countries, traveled the world with other disciples, and spent weekends hopping to different cities and worshipping in various congregations. I lived life to the fullest as Jesus has promised (John 10:10), and the most amazing thing happened along this journey. My desire for a relationship did not disappear, but it no longer held the power over me that it once did. For me, a relationship had become an idol. If only I had that right relationship, then my life would be... what? Complete? Fulfilled? Joyous? Filled with love? These longings were not at all bad, it was just that I was placing too much on this relationship. I was looking to this relationship to fulfill longings that can only be filled by God. My engagement in ministry shattered this idol. I felt fulfilled in ways I never thought I could apart from companionship, and I realized that if God kept me single for the rest of my life that I could trust him to make it completely fulfilling. I also realized that my previous loathing over my single stage of life was a self-fulfilling prophecy. I sat around with a miserable attitude, so I became miserable. Then I took that as evidence that singlehood was miserable. What foolishness.

Once I started living my single life in the way Paul described, I realized just how incredible of a gift I was given. It did not remove my desire to be in a relationship, but it put it in a proper perspective, and with that I could avoid the tendency I had to idolize the married stage of life. I still struggled with loneliness but used those feelings as fuel for my prayer life and to draw closer to God in those moments. The result was that it strengthened my relationship with God and strengthened my ministry. I look back on my single stage of life with fondness and no regrets. I was able to use that time productively for God's kingdom, was able to help many know Christ, was able to grow in my knowledge of God's Word and was able to experience such beautiful moments with brothers and sisters both in the United States and abroad, to God be the glory. This was what my singleness gifted me. I am a richer, more faithful person because of my single stage of life. My closest friendships down to this day were made in this stage of life. There is nothing like shared experiences, shared goals, and shared ministry to build deep and lasting friendships. I still lean on these friendships to this day.

So, there is an opportunity here. Singlehood can be a self-fulfilling prophecy of misery and loneliness, or it can be a vibrant expanse of faith, relationships, ministry to the Lord, and the witness of spiritual fruit growing in your lives and ministries. How will you use this stage of life? How will you use your time? Your autonomy? Will it be used to build your own personal kingdom, or to be devoted to God's kingdom? Will you squander it away, or use it to propel you into a life of God-filled ambitions? A life of undivided devotion to the Lord?

What Undivided Devotion Can Build

I have seen singles make massive strides in various aspects of their lives as they have used their time and autonomy to pursue various goals. I have seen singles make large leaps in their careers, or in their physical fitness, or in their travel/social lives. These strides are made because these things have become their primary focus, and it is only reasonable to expect to see progress in what we devote our time and resources towards. Now what would it look like if a larger percentage of single disciples made their singles ministry their primary focus? Made the Gospel their primary focus? Now consider if a larger percentage of singles not just made ministry and the Gospel their primary focus, but submitted their powers and crowns for this express purpose? Now their money, their time, their skills, their energy, their networks, their education, their all is being used to proclaim Christ to the world. What would your singles ministry look like if you and other single disciples took hold of it, and invested your undivided devotion towards it?

It is important to make clear that this is not to discount those pursuing other ambitions. There will always be those who feel called to pursue different goals for their lives, and this does not make one unspiritual or less of a Christian for doing so. There are those who have career aspirations or find fitness or education to be high priorities in their lives. I would not discount this outright. The right question to ask is what would it look like for them to use the power of those aspirations in undivided worship to the Lord? What would our singles ministries look like if single disciples used the advancement in their careers to fund missions? What if single disciples used their pursuit of physical fitness or education as gifts to build up the body of Christ, and to evangelize in the process?

It is not wrong to pursue goals, but it is wrong to abandon your duty towards ministry. I see this trend more in singles ministry than in any other ministry. The ministry becomes a secondary consideration, or no consideration at all. Disciples stop participating, stop attending, stop engaging. Various reasons are given. Too busy, not feeling it, it is just not interesting, or no reason is given at all. This simply means that ministry is not a priority, and our powers and crowns are to be used for the god and kingdom of self instead of for the real God and his real kingdom. It certainly is not the attitude from Scripture. This is where the opportunity for undivided devotion to God becomes undivided devotion to myself, my career, my plans, ME. What a waste. I find that Satan has dragged many singles into this exact state of mind. Is it possible Satan knows just how powerful this group could be if it would just orient its focus back on the affairs of God?

Not a Zero-Sum Game

The beauty of all of this is that it is not a zero-sum game, as we can often believe. "Does this mean that I have to give up my career to build ministry?" It might mean that, but most often I have found that it does not. I certainly would have you take a close look at whatever you feel you could not give up for God, because that may have become an idol in your heart. But for the most part, I have found that many singles who make ministry a focus, are also able to thrive in their careers, are also able to make it to the gym, or pursue any number of other goals, while still giving their all for God.

I can remember a particular point as a single man where God was working abundantly in my personal ministry. There were seven people who wanted to study the Bible and know about Jesus, which was incredible. This was an incredibly busy time of my life. I was leading the singles ministry in my home congregation, was organizing a teacher's group within the church, working on my masters, and working my full-time job. I want to emphasize that this was not a typical experience, nor was it sustainable over the long term. I do not recommend running yourself into the ground or overextending yourself, nor do I consider it a mark of righteousness to do so. But in this particular juncture of my life, the mission field was ripe, and as the opportunities presented themselves, it was an incredible chance to see God work powerfully across multiple passions at once. There is no way I could even attempt this as a married man. It would be to the neglect of ministry to my family, and likely to the detriment of my well-being.

Yet in that time of my life, I saw how God sustained me, and allowed me to work across these multiple pursuits. The fruit of this was that people were baptized and restored to Christ, I was able to thrive in my workplace and in my classes, and I saw Christ being formed little by little in myself and in the ministries I served in. I do not share this to elevate myself, but to elevate God. This was *"the grace of God that was with me"* (1 Corinthians 15:10), and this same grace will work powerfully through you too. My work with ministry did not mean I had to abandon my masters (Ironically, I did have to abandon it when I got married, but by God's grace, he has returned me to these studies recently!). My work with ministry did not mean that I was unable to thrive at work either. We often present ourselves with these false binaries ("If I do ministry, then I won't have time for...") and use this as the excuse for why we will not give our best to God. Placing ministry first does not necessarily mean that you must abandon your other goals (though it is certainly possible that God will call you to do exactly that). But even if this were the case, I question whether we truly understand the true worth of things, when we balk at engaging in the eternal work so that we may elevate the temporary. When we do this, we are like the twenty-four elders gripping their crowns with one hand and hugging their thrones with the other, refusing to give up either despite being in the presence of the one who gave them their thrones, and their crowns, not to mention the air they breathe, the life they live, and the light of salvation that makes this scene possible in the first place.

The main point here is to rid us of the fallacy that we cannot pursue multiple priorities at once. But even if this were not true, I hope you can see how even your ambitions can be the power you submit in undivided devotion to the Lord. To use your very ambitions to further his kingdom and build up his body which is his Church.

View From the Other Side

The truth is that there is urgency for your devotion to God in ministry. It is not just true that the Church needs you, it is also true that this undivided focus on the affairs of God is something that you need as well. We are called to live and serve in community: *"From him the whole body, joined and held together by every supporting ligament, grows and builds itself up in love, as **each part does its work**."* Ephesians 4:16 (emphasis added). But I wish to share a perspective that I hope will help frame your own thinking about the single stage of life.

After about a decade of living as a single disciple of Christ, I was married to an incredible woman of God, and became a stepdad to two amazing boys. I certainly believe that God used my ministry experiences to prepare me for such a role, and I am grateful for the challenges, victories and defeats I experienced serving in this capacity, for they all helped refine me. Yet one of the biggest takeaways I had after being married was the simple fact that 1 Corinthians 7:33-34 was true: *"But a married man is concerned about the affairs of this world—how he can please his wife—34and his interests are divided."* I used to teach this passage as a single man, yet I did not understand just how true this passage was until I got married. Of course, being married with children is different than being married without children, but the conclusion remains the same. In marriage, your family becomes your ministry, whether this includes a spouse, or a spouse and children. You must take care of this family that God has given you. What I underestimated was just how much this would impact my ability to engage in ministry. Before marriage, I estimated that I would only be able to do half as much ministry work as I could as a single man. This estimation proved to be way off. I was quite shocked to see how giving in even 20% of the way I did as a single man was a challenge. My time was now divided, and I was experiencing it firsthand. Paul communicated as much when he mentioned the divided nature of a married man, but until experiencing it for myself I did not fully grasp the disparity between what I could do as a single man compared to what I could do as a married man with children. If you go on to get married, then you will find that the window to serve in this undivided way has closed. That is not to say that the married person cannot glorify God, engage in the work of ministry, or serve in incredible ways. A new opportunity of learning to serve as a united pair is presented in marriage. I am amazed at the examples of service, and selflessness I have seen in many married brothers and sisters. It is just that a married person is necessarily and rightly divided in their attention, and this is what Paul was trying to encourage us with. The opportunity presented to you as a single man or woman is like no other, and once you are married, that opportunity has closed. You will continue to minister before God, but your ministry will shift to include this ministry of family, and so you will be divided.

Every married person will have their own unique situation, yet I have yet to meet a disciple who has said that marriage has provided them more time to engage in ministry. I can imagine scenarios where this might be true (for example if one spouse works, and the other does not), but I have not come across too many situations like this. The truth is that when we engage in the ministry of family as a married person, the things we could do before are reduced. The single stage of life provides an opportunity like no other to be devoted to the work of ministry. Do not waste this chance.

If we are to accept the gift that this stage of life is affording us, then we must understand the gift properly, we must define it properly, understand its worth properly, and for all that to happen we must let go of the lies that we have allowed to define this gift for us. These lies have caused us to devalue this gift, misunderstand this gift, and therefore dismiss this gift. It is your job as a single disciple to replace the lie with the truth that it has undermined.

Reflections on Powers and Crowns in Your Life

The first section of this book presented 1 Corinthians 7:25-35 and provided some reflections on that passage of Scripture. I encourage you to re-read that section and consider this passage of Scripture. Afterwards, take some time to consider and pray through the following questions:

1. Do I really believe that I am in a blessed state of life, and have a unique opportunity?

2. Do I see the value of my singlehood, and understand the opportunity I have to submit this power to God?

3. What would it look like for me to have undivided devotion to the affairs of the Lord? To submit my powers and crowns to him and his kingdom?

4. What unique calling do I have in God's kingdom?

5. What would it look like if I committed along with the single disciples in my local church to build a ministry based on the premise of this gift of singleness? What could we accomplish? What would it look like?

For some, the single stage of life will only last for a short while. That is the window you have to use this gift to its utmost potential. What would singles ministries look like if the members would only believe this Biblical truth? Many singles believe that the single stage of life has two primary purposes: to pursue your career and find a spouse. These are not bad goals to have. Pursue that extra degree that will propel you in your career, work hard at your jobs as if you were working in the name of the Lord (Colossians 3:17), and yes, go on dates with disciples of Christ, build quality pure friendships with the opposite sex, and look for that spouse that you believe you can build a life in Christ with. But consider that as important as these things are, they remain secondary to your devotion to God. The opportunity you have to conduct your own personal ministry for God is like no other, and what you build now as a single Christian, is what you will carry into your future, whether that be a life of marriage, or a life of ever-growing and ever-maturing devotion to God as a single man or woman.

CHAPTER THREE

Ownership of the Body of Christ

In the previous chapter, we outlined a Bible-defined identity and purpose for single disciples and discussed the tremendous opportunities that this stage of life holds. But what comes next? This is where we turn our attention to building a foundation from which to launch a renewed vision for singles ministry.

Ownership

The first thing you would expect to see in a singles ministry that has embraced its Biblical identity is ownership. That is to say that the members of the ministry would take ownership of the ministry as a whole. It is also to say that the larger church body would also take ownership of the ministry, since we are all one body (this will be discussed in greater detail in the next chapter).

The question of ownership can be slightly deceptive. Just because we belong to a group does not mean that we have taken ownership of it. Oftentimes, the dynamic that can manifest is that group ownership is taken on by the group leaders, and then all the rest become mere participants. Participation is a good thing. It is certainly better than not showing up at all. But participating and taking ownership are quite different. A simple illustration should suffice. Say I was part of a singles household, and I wanted to encourage my neighbors who were going through some tough times. I decide that the way I would like to do so would be to prepare a nice dinner and invite both my roommates and neighbors to join. This act of service is one that I have created and own. What will be on the dinner menu, how the table will be decorated, the time of the dinner, and all other details will be dictated at my discretion. Its success or failure will depend entirely on my efforts. In essence, I both lead and own this event.

However, let us say that while I am cooking, a member of my household sees me working away in the kitchen and then offers to help me prepare the meal. At that point, this individual has moved beyond being a participant in the meal and has now become co-owners or co-creator of this meal alongside me. Say another member of the household offers to clean up afterwards. They too have taken a piece of the ownership of that evening's events. While my roommates could have just shown up at dinner time, enjoyed the meal, and then headed back to their respective rooms when it was over, they actually took part in creating that evening. This illustrates the difference between ownership and participation. Participating allows you to show up, enjoy and leave. Owning means you put in the work. It did not change the fact perhaps that I was leading the event, or that the event was my initial idea, once my roommates got involved, we were creating the dinner together. It is easy to look at our singles ministry leaders and expect them to take on the ownership of the ministry, but that will only limit how much they can do, and what the group can do. The more members of a group take ownership, the more can be accomplished. Ownership is not the same as leadership. It is not helpful to have 50 different leaders all trying to dictate a vision and direction. It would be chaotic. However, it is incredibly helpful to have 50 different owners, who can work alongside leaders to help make a vision for ministry a reality. Good leadership is a collaboration with owners.

We know that we have all been gifted by the Holy Spirit to serve the ministry (1 Corinthians 12), and that we are constantly being equipped for good works (Ephesians 4:11–13). Therefore, there is no role in the Church whose job description reads "just show up." We are to be those who contribute and help build. There is an incredible example of this in the book of Exodus we will reflect on in this chapter.

Imagine for a moment that you were an Israelite enslaved in Egypt, and you have just borne witness to the ten plagues, the escape from Egypt, being trapped along the Red Sea by the Egyptian army, only to witness the incredible miracle of the parting of the Red Sea. You then watched as the Egyptian army that you had no possible way of defeating, was drowned in the Red Sea. Completely defeated without you or your people having to shoot a single arrow. You are now standing on the opposite shore, facing a vast desert wilderness. What you have with you are the animals you shepherded, and the articles of clothes, silver, and gold you had been given by your Egyptian neighbors as you fled the country (Exodus 12:35–36). These items were likely your first taste of wealth, and as Scripture tells us, God had made the Egyptians favorably disposed towards you so that they would give you these belongings. In other words, these possessions were a gift from God. Wandering this desert landscape, you are certain that whatever items you lose, cannot be replaced. What you have is what you have, and apart from bartering with your fellow Israelites, this is all you can hope to have for as long as you are in this wilderness. Then one day, Moses comes with a unique request. He says that God has asked you all to build a tabernacle, provided the exact dimensions and descriptions of everything that was to be made. Moses is asking you to participate in this project. Let us pick up the story here in Exodus 35:4–10:

> ⁴Moses said to the whole Israelite community, "This is what the LORD has commanded: ⁵From what you have, take an offering for the LORD. Everyone who is willing is to bring to the LORD an offering of gold, silver and bronze; ⁶blue, purple and scarlet yarn and fine linen; goat hair; ⁷ram skins dyed red and another type of durable leather; acacia wood; ⁸olive oil for the light; spices for the anointing oil and for the fragrant incense; ⁹and onyx stones and other gems to be mounted on the

ephod and breastpiece.

   ¹⁰"All who are skilled among you are to come and make everything the LORD has commanded."

Here we see Moses request that the Israelites do two things. First, for those who were willing, to take from what they had and make an offering for the Lord. Second, he asks that those who are skilled, to use their talents to make the things God has asked them to create. It must be emphasized that this offering was for *"Everyone who is willing"* (v. 5). That is to say that it was not a tax on the people, or a compulsory collection, it was to be given freely.

So now you have a choice to make. You had lived in poverty as a slave, but as you fled Egypt you were given an abundance of possessions. It was your first real taste of a better life. Perhaps you had hoped to use these possessions to establish your home in the promised land. Or to give to your future children. Or to trade for something different that you had always dreamed for but did not have. And here, God was asking you to depart from these items that you had already placed some of your future or present hopes in. You know that whatever you give, you will not be able to replace in that desert. What you give is gone.

What happens next is quite remarkable. Not only do the Israelites give of their resources, skills, and time, they give so much of themselves that Moses has to restrain them from giving more.

Exodus 36:3-7

³They received from Moses all the offerings the Israelites had brought to carry out the work of constructing the sanctuary. And the people continued to bring freewill offerings morning after morning. ⁴So all the skilled workers who were doing all the work on the sanctuary left what they were doing ⁵and said to Moses, "The people are bringing more than enough for doing the work the LORD commanded to be done."

⁶Then Moses gave an order and they sent this word throughout the camp: "No man or woman is to make anything else as an offering for the sanctuary." And so the people were restrained from bringing more, ⁷because what they already had was more than enough to do all the work.

So much was being given that it became a burden to the people doing the work. Too much time was needed to manage everything that was being given that the work itself could not be done. If only this was the problem we faced today! Morning after morning the people were bringing their free will offerings until they were commanded to stop. Even though they likely could not replace the items they gave, the Israelites continued to give it away in great abundance. What would motivate them to give so sacrificially?

These Israelites were given an opportunity of a lifetime to build the very dwelling place where God would reside among them. To be able to participate in that was surely of great motivation. But there is something more. Yes, the items they gave away were likely to not be replaced, but going forward, every time they looked at the tabernacle, they would see the very items they gave woven into the dwelling place of God. They could point to the gold they contributed, they could point to the skins they gave, they could look at the skillful work they had put in and know deep in their hearts that I was a part of that. The Israelites got to participate in building something God would use to make his presence known on earth. What an incredible privilege this was! Can you imagine the feeling those Israelites had when the work was done and they watched as *"the cloud covered the tent of meeting, and the glory of the LORD filled the tabernacle."* (Exodus 40:34)? Conversely, imagine if you were one of the people who could not bear to part with your belongings. Who did not want to give of your own free will, who perhaps reasoned away that there will be other times to give or serve God. To then watch the glory of the LORD fill the tabernacle that you could not be bothered to help build. Imagine the feeling of that. Would you feel a sense of loss? Of regret? This was an opportunity like no other to participate in the purposes of the Divine, and it was missed.

The Israelites took ownership of this responsibility. They were given a purpose to fulfill, and they did so with incredible enthusiasm. They were asked to give, but only if they were willing. There would be no compulsion, or force used, simply a request, and they were found to be more than willing. As a result, they were able to participate in the construction of the tabernacle of God, where he would live in their midst. The Israelites did not delegate the giving to the leaders, they did not disregard the task because they felt they had more important things to do, they did not look to their own desires and plans for what they wanted to do with the gifts God had given them, they instead gave sacrificially, worked earnestly, and created something incredible that honored God and made his presence known on Earth.

Let us consider what this story tells us about ownership. It did not matter what role each person had. Some administered, some gave, some worked, but all created, all contributed and therefore all participated in building the very dwelling place of God. This purpose and ministry united them, and they came together in their willingness to serve God. Because of their willingness and sacrifice, something incredible was built by their hands that God blessed.

The reason this story comes to mind is that there are some interesting parallels between the Israelites then and the call of Christians today. As the Israelites were called to build a tabernacle where God would dwell, so we are called to build a temple where God will dwell as well:

Ephesians 2:19-22

[19]Consequently, you are no longer foreigners and strangers, but fellow citizens with God's people and also members of his household, [20]built on the foundation of the apostles and prophets, with

Christ Jesus himself as the chief cornerstone. [21]In him the whole building is joined together and rises to become a holy temple in the Lord. [22]***And in him you too are being built together to become a dwelling in which God lives by his Spirit.*** (Emphasis Added).

The Israelites were called to the purpose of building the tabernacle, and to use whatever they had, be it their possessions or their skills, to contribute for that purpose. Consider this compared to what it tells us in Ephesians 4:11–13:

[11]So Christ himself gave the apostles, the prophets, the evangelists, the pastors and teachers, [12]to equip his people for works of service, so that the body of Christ may be built up [13]until we all reach unity in the faith and in the knowledge of the Son of God and become mature, attaining to the whole measure of the fullness of Christ.

This passage tells us that God appoints some to specific positions (apostles, prophets, evangelists, pastors, and teachers) for a specific purpose: to equip his people for works of service. Some engage in the equipping (who themselves must be equipped for such a ministry), others are meant to be equipped and start doing the things they are being equipped to do: works of service. The purpose of this is "so that the body of Christ may be built up" (v. 12), which is a task that is ongoing *"until we all reach unity in the faith and in the knowledge of the Son of God and become mature, attaining to the whole measure of the fullness of Christ."* (v. 13). The implication is that we are all meant to be working towards this unity, and that together we strive in attaining to the fullness of Christ. We work together, united in purpose towards this end, equipping, being equipped and completing works of service. The point is driven further in Romans 12:4–8:

> [4]For just as each of us has one body with many members, and these members do not all have the same function, [5]so in Christ we, though many, form one body, and each member belongs to all the others. [6]We have different gifts, according to the grace given to each of us. If your gift is prophesying, then prophesy in accordance with your faith; [7]if it is serving, then serve; if it is teaching, then teach; [8]if it is to encourage, then give encouragement; if it is giving, then give generously; if it is to lead, do it diligently; if it is to show mercy, do it cheerfully.

Romans encourages us with the idea that we are one body with many members, and that the various members do not have the same function. We are diverse in how we can contribute to the body of Christ, yet regardless of what our individual gift(s) may be, we are to use them towards this purpose. The passage therefore reminds us that in Christ, we no longer belong to ourselves but that *"each member belongs to all the others."* (v. 5). We belong to one another and are therefore reliant on each other. That is why we need each member to do its part.

Consider the implications of this to our discussion of ownership. We are building up the dwelling place of God, by which he will be made known on this Earth. That is what the body of Christ, his holy Church is. Just as by God's provision, the Israelites were gifted possessions as they entered their freedom from Egypt, so we are provided spiritual gifts as we enter our freedom in Christ. As the Israelites were asked to give back from these gifts for the construction of the dwelling place of God, we too are being asked to give of our gifts to build up the dwelling place of God. You are needed, you are valued, and you are essential to this picture. We are like lights that shine the brightest when we shine together. God could have chosen any place to dwell through his Holy Spirit. He is choosing you, and he has chosen us to be his holy temple here on Earth. What an incredible privilege this is.

If the church is the body of Christ, and the dwelling place of God through the Holy Spirit, what happens when only part of the body is attaining to the fullness of Christ while the other part sits idle? What happens when the body is equipped with an abundance of members with unique gifts, but those members do not contribute or are barely present? What work can be done? What sort of unity can be built? What fullness of Christ can be attained? And what effect does this have for those who are trying to do this work? It can be so disheartening for them. The inactivity of the many will hinder the work of the few. That is not how ministry is to be.

Why do I bring this up? Because singlehood, and its tendency to pursue self, consumes the ministries that are made to serve them. Singles ministry, and single disciples are the toughest to get ownership from. Single disciples can be quick to abandon the ministry they are in, because they do not find it lively enough, interesting enough, or simply find their own pursuits of greater import. What this attitude betrays is a lack of ownership, which manifests in a lack of participation, lack of interest, and therefore lack of growth. This runs counter to what undivided devotion to the Lord should look like. Once you have submitted your powers and crowns, you must take up the ministry of building up the body of Christ. You, like the Israelites of the past, are building the dwelling place of God here on earth. This is not a ministry to be taken lightly. It is not a ministry to devalue, and dash against the rocks of your disinterest. It is a ministry to take hold of firmly and throw all of yourself towards, giving of your skill, your administration, your resources to watch it come to fruition, so that one day you too can point at the body that has been built and see your contributions present within them. What an incredible privilege this is! When you see the people you share the Gospel with put their faith in Christ, and then see them engaging and serving in the fellowship, you are seeing manifest before your very eyes the fruit of your sacrifice of time and effort in the body of Christ. You see it when your skills and talents bring together events that benefit and mature the body, and watch Christ be formed a little more in your brothers and sisters as a result. You see it when your acts of service and good works elevate the name of Christ in your community and forges you a little more into the likeness of Christ. We are seeing the temple built around us, and we have the privilege to contribute to its construction of our own free will, but are you willing?

Undivided devotion to God means that you are taking ownership of the ministry that God is calling you to do. Taking ownership of the specific calling and instruction God provides you by his Word, living out his commands to the fullest of your abilities, and participating with God in the construction of Christ's body is an incredible privilege. Do you treat this privilege with disdain? Or do you treat it as the incredible gift that it truly is?

It is time to leave behind our disinterested attitudes. It is time to stop valuing our powers and crowns over and above the power and crown of our Lord Jesus Christ. It is time to stop treating our call to ministry with disdain. If this has been your attitude in the past, the beauty of our relationship with God is the incredible gifts of grace and repentance that he offers us. We can repent and embrace the biblical identity of singlehood, so that we can see the power of this stage of life fully take hold.

What Taking Ownership Looks Like

We have discussed the necessity of taking ownership, but it remains to be explained what taking ownership looks like. This is going to look different for each person in terms of their individual gifts, so this advice is necessarily given at the big picture level. I believe there are a few things you can do to take ownership of your ministry right now:

1) Pray to God for your singles ministry, your church, and for God to reveal ways that you can serve your singles ministry.

2) Ask the leaders of your singles ministry how you can serve and help build the ministry. The leaders should have a pulse on what is going on in your ministry. Ask what the needs are, and how you can meet them. Ask if there are any Bible studies you can jump into, and if not, ask how you can assist in the evangelistic efforts. As a former singles ministry leader, I can speak from experience that members who look to remove some of the burden of the work of ministry are a God send.

3) Ask the leaders of your local congregation how you can help meet needs in the body. It is great to be able to build your singles ministry, but the beauty of having undivided devotion is that you may find yourself flexible enough to meet multiple needs at the same time. Maybe there is a need for ushering, or in leading worship, or perhaps there are members who are sick and shut in that you could go visit and encourage. See what opportunities to serve lie within the larger body you worship.

4) Lastly, consider your skills, abilities, and interests, and then consider the needs you see in your singles ministry or larger church community. Do you see any needs that you

can meet with the skills or abilities you have? Sometimes God will put a particular need on your heart that others do not see. This is a ministry calling for you. Discuss the need with those who lead the ministry, and more importantly, provide the solution. It can be overwhelming for those leading a ministry to have members tell them all about the needs, and then leave it in their hands to deal with. The ministry requires every member to do their part.

5) Talk to another brother and sister in your ministry and bring them along to do the same. It is great to call yourself higher, and repent in your attitude towards ministry, but it is also necessary to call others to take on the same attitude. We need to encourage our brothers and sisters to join us in embracing our identity and taking ownership of the ministry, and this starts by calling another brother or sister to join you in this pursuit. In this way, we call one another higher.

This is a short list, but I have seen how these five steps set Christians on a course for giving, building, and taking ownership of their respective ministries. Just imagine if your ministry leaders gained 3 more disciples asking these questions, and calling other singles to do the same? What if this number was even 10 or 20? Could you imagine 20 individuals praying for their ministry, and using their undivided devotion, their powers, their crowns to meet needs in the community and spread the Gospel? What would your ministry look like if this were so? Now imagine if the vast majority of your ministry was rooted in this conviction. It is incredible to think about the amazing works, and manifestations of the

Holy Spirit we would see with that much undivided devotion whole-heartedly dedicated to building their ministries and churches. It all starts with you, and your decision to take ownership of your ministry.

If your ministry already looks like this, then amen! Praise God for the convictions and maturity that has been built within you. Continue to walk in those ways and inspire others to do the same. The body of Christ will be edified through your faith and efforts, and the communities you live in will come to know Jesus Christ through your testimony. This is the goal and the vision, to be more effective for God for the sake of the Gospel.

If your ministry does not look like this, then amen! You can always start down this path, and help be part of the creation of such a ministry. Do not be afraid to be the first. Do not be afraid to start something. God will move according to your faith, and there is much good in exploring what you can contribute to the body of Christ.

Ownership, Then What?

Engaging in the 5 steps listed above is a great place to start exploring how you can be your most for God, build the body of Christ, and take ownership of your ministry. A group of singles committed to taking ownership of their singles ministry and submitting their powers and crowns to do so already eliminates some of the greatest hindrances to ministry. But once you have made the decision to own your singles ministry, have engaged in the work of ministry, and have brought along other brothers and sisters to do the same, then what? Is there a prototypical ministry to model after? The short answer is no. Each ministry will look different based on the culture they are in, the size of the group they have, the gifts of the members involved, the faith of the individuals, and any number of other factors that impact and influence the make-up of a group. This is the beauty of taking ownership of your ministry: you now own it. It is an obvious conclusion, but after you have taken ownership, you now have to own it! This is where joining together with your single leaders, church leaders and your ministries in prayer can help forge a vision for your specific group. As owners, it is not just on you to seek God for how you can contribute to the body, but also to work with others in your group and with the leaders who watch over you to forge a vision together.

Ownership at the Community Level

We have discussed the need for ministry ownership from single disciples, but we will now turn our attention to the ownership needed from the larger church community. The ownership of a particular ministry does not belong just to that ministry alone. The teens do not exist in a separate body from the marrieds, nor do the campus and singles sit in a body apart from the teens. We together form the body of Christ, and each part belongs to the others. *"so in Christ we, though many, form one body, and **each member belongs to all the others.**"* (Emphasis Added) Romans 12:5. This means that we are not just responsible for ourselves, or our ministries, we are also responsible for the body as a whole. As a community of believers, we can commit the error of turning a blind eye to the needs of the very brothers and sisters who worship right beside us. The needs of any ministry do not exist apart from the larger body. Paul's words regarding the body of Christ are instructive here:

1 Corinthians 12:21-26

[21]The eye cannot say to the hand, "I don't need you!" And the head cannot say to the feet, "I don't need you!" [22]On the contrary, those parts of the body that seem to be weaker are indispensable, [23]and the parts that we think are less honorable we treat with special honor. And the parts that are unpresentable are treated with special modesty,[24] while our presentable parts need no special treatment. But God has put the body together, giving greater honor to the parts that lacked it, [25]so that there should be no division in the body, **but that its parts should have equal concern for each other.** [26]If one part suffers, every part suffers with it; if one part is honored, every part rejoices with it. (Emphasis Added).

The passage tells us how God places the body together, elevating those that need elevating, giving special treatment to the parts that need it, balancing between the parts to create a body where *"there should be no division... that its parts should* have equal concern for each other" (v. 25). The passage is clear that we should have "equal" concern for each other, and as a result of this equal concern we should have a body where *"If one part suffers, every part suffers with it; if one part is honored, every part rejoices with it."* (v. 26). This is where we as Christians have an opportunity to grow. If we can acknowledge that our singles ministries have been struggling, some of which have been struggling for years, but are not stepping in to provide the support and strength our brothers and sisters need, then we are falling short in our practice of this passage.

I have witnessed church communities wrap their arms around ministries that are struggling. I have seen disciples rally together to help sustain and build their teen ministries. I have seen impassioned speeches given about the state of their campus ministries, and have seen a call to rally our resources, increase contributions, ask for volunteers to help build up our campuses. This is a beautiful practice that benefits our churches greatly. It brings attention to the needs and rallies the church to meet those needs. However, I wonder how many of these sorts of rallies and impassioned calls for action are considered for the singles ministry? I have unfortunately never seen such a call for this ministry (though that is not to say they do not happen). It simply brings us back to the question of whether we are showing equal concern for our single brothers and sisters.

The quality of church ownership can manifest in various ways, but not the least of which is the strategies employed for singles ministry. Many churches have not allocated full time staff to singles ministry, and there can be real financial barriers to doing so. Instead, the most common model I have seen used is where singles are called to lead themselves. This is an idea I agree with. I think that many groups of single disciples have the maturity, experience, and gifts to do exactly that. But what tends to happen is that when needs throughout the body arise, singles are often called in to fill them. So, when campus needs strengthening, or there is a desire to expand that ministry, single leaders are recruited to join up with the campus. When teens need extra volunteers to build up that ministry, single leaders are once again recruited to join that ministry. This is often done even when those ministries have full time staff resources already devoted to them. That means that our singles ministries are often drained of their leadership, but still expected to lead themselves. If we were to sit down today and ask the question "What is the best way to build a singles ministry?" I am certain that this is not the strategy that we would come up with. Yet it is often the strategy that is used. Why? We have to question why we would use a strategy that simply does not work. Meanwhile, the opportunity to spread the Gospel to this ever-growing demographic is slipping through our fingers.

It bears mentioning that teens and campus are groups that typically cannot lead themselves effectively. They need the leadership, wisdom, experience, and energy of people who have moved beyond those stages of life. It makes sense to have staff allocated to these groups, and it makes sense to have support to help build them. But if we remove those singles gifted in leadership from the singles ministry, how can that ministry then lead themselves? Do you see the problem? This is perhaps where our cultural influence manifests and gets the better of us. We would never build any ministry like this, but this is how we oftentimes approach singles ministry. Then we can also stand back and wonder why the singles ministry struggles. We are not seeing the fruits of a weak and struggling ministry, we are seeing the fruits of a weak strategy. This is where we have an opportunity to grow and start taking ownership of our single brothers and sisters. We need to begin expressing equal concern for our brothers and sisters, and not remain aloof to their needs or the condition of their ministry.

In using singles to lead in our other ministries and initiatives, we have already acknowledged the value they bring. This is partly why I believe there is a tremendous opportunity within the singles ministry that is being lost. I believe they have the potential to be one of the strongest parts of the body of Christ. With a new vision that embraces a biblical identity for this stage of life, we can begin to see this group thrive. I fear that as far as the body analogy goes, the singles ministry is a part that we have allowed to atrophy based on a ministry strategy that has excluded them. If we are pulling singles to support other ministry initiatives, just imagine if we invested and grew our singles ministries? Could you imagine how many more singles could be available to lead all sorts of initiatives within the Church? Perhaps we are missing an opportunity to build something that can be a major blessing not just to singles in our communities, but to the Church as a whole, and to the ever-growing single population in this world that needs to hear their message and see their example of Christ.

This is where we need to take our responsibilities as brothers, sisters, shepherds, and fellow members of the body of Christ seriously, and ensure that we are doing the most we can do before our God to care for his body. I think as a Church it is good to ask, are we doing everything within our power to strengthen the singles the way we do for the other members of our body? If we can invest in staff, interns, trainings, and workshops for other ministries, can we invest in our singles to make sure their spiritual needs are being met as well? Can we grow them so that out of their abundance they can support our other ministry initiatives effectively, while still meeting the needs of their own ministry, and proclaiming the Gospel to the singles in our communities?

If we see anything from the Exodus passages shared earlier in this chapter, it is how the community pulled together to build something that would bring glory to God. If we are to build strong singles ministries, singles need to own a large part of that. But the church community also must own this as well. United together, we can build church communities that meet the needs of all the members. In so doing, we will be stronger.

Ownership and showing equal concern within the body of Christ will help situate our churches to start edifying the entire body and ensure that we strengthen ourselves in full and not in part. It is not simply a matter of financial allocation, as if money alone can build ministry. We need ministries built on the Holy Spirit. The Holy Spirit works through those who are willing to be used by him. Consider that Scripture tells us that you can quench the Holy Spirit (1 Thessalonians 5:19), you can grieve the Holy Spirit (Ephesians 4:30), you can resist the Holy Spirit (Acts 7:51). What is the condition of the Holy Spirit inside of you? The next chapter is a call to action to build up our singles within the body of Christ to live their fullest for God and have a ministry that shows the world what undivided devotion to the affairs of the Lord looks like. It is time to stamp out the unbiblical cultural influences that can devalue singles in Christian communities. It is time to take ownership. Before beginning the next chapter, take time to pray that the Holy Spirit may prompt your heart towards the actions you should take, and to have the courage and faith to follow through. Alone we are nothing, but you *"can do all this through him who gives me strength."* (Philippians 4:13).

CHAPTER FOUR

Not a Matter of Talk, but of Power

1 Corinthians 4:20

"For the kingdom of God is not a matter of talk but of power."

We have endeavored thus far to promote a vision of our singles ministries that aligns with scriptural teaching concerning the single stage of life. A vision where singles in our churches do not feel overlooked or undervalued, but are instead given worth, trust and investment. A vision where singles do not see their singleness as a liability, but as a powerful opportunity to invest in God's kingdom. Where singles ministries are not viewed as a place holder for those who "failed" to get married, but as a ministry of power, purpose, and passion. A vision where marriage is not idolized, or elevated above singlehood, but where the two are honored in their proper respects and given the dignity God allots to them both. We should not build churches where our college students dread entering their singles ministries, because they see a "dead" ministry. Many reading this will agree with these statements and give their emphatic "amens!" Yet this will all amount to nothing if we do not take proper action. Through faith-filled actions we can see the Holy Spirit move and we can see God's hand at work. That way, this conversation will not end with mere words, but with a manifestation of God's power.

A practical guide on building singles ministries would be a book project on its own, and perhaps if God wills it so, such a project can become the follow up to this book. We do not have enough space here to explore all those lessons. We can, however, discuss here how individual congregations can begin the work of (re)building their singles ministries. This is a call to action to start having these discussions and to start making a commitment to building stronger ministries. It is directed at evangelists, elders, teachers, church leaders, church members, singles, marrieds, and all who bear the name of Christ. For as we learned in the previous chapter, we all bear the responsibility of the body of Christ, and each of us belong to the others (Romans 12:5). Together with the Holy Spirit, we can change the course of our singles ministries, and build communities that honor the teachings of 1 Corinthians 7:32–35. We can build communities of singles who have surrendered their powers and crowns and have committed the single stage of life in undivided devotion to God, and to the affairs of the Lord.

The action steps below are inspired by the events of Haggai 1, and the lessons we can draw from these passages of Scripture. Let us turn to Haggai for a quick devotional lesson to inspire our next steps towards this vision for our singles ministries.

Call to Action: Lessons from the Prophet Haggai

The book of Ezra relays the story of how the Jewish people who had come out of exile in Babylon were endeavoring to rebuild the temple of God. It is an inspiring story in its depiction of a group of people who committed themselves to a rather lofty and inspiring plan, and yet fell short in following through with their actions. Although they had come together to rebuild Jerusalem, and the temple of God, they had put the latter project on pause as they began to focus on building their respective homes. After the construction of God's Holy Temple had been delayed for quite some time, God began to speak to the prophet Haggai giving him a message to relay to his people. We will begin reading in Haggai chapter one.

Action Step 1: Give Careful Thought to Your Ways

Haggai 1:2-11

²This is what the LORD Almighty says: "These people say, 'The time has not yet come to rebuild the LORD's house.'"

³Then the word of the LORD came through the prophet Haggai: ⁴'Is it a time for you yourselves to be living in your paneled houses, while this house remains a ruin?'

⁵Now this is what the LORD Almighty says:

'Give careful thought to your ways.' ⁶You have planted much, but harvested little. You eat, but never have enough. You drink, but never have your fill. You put on clothes, but are not warm. You earn wages, only to put them in a purse with holes in it.'

⁷This is what the LORD Almighty says: **'Give careful thought to your ways.'** Go up into the mountains and bring down timber and build my house, so that I may take pleasure in it and be honored," says the LORD. ⁹"You expected much, but see, it turned out to be little. What you brought home, I blew away. Why?" declares the LORD Almighty. "Because of my house, which remains a ruin, while each of you is busy with your own house. ¹⁰Therefore, because of you the heavens have withheld their dew and the earth its crops. ¹¹I called for a drought on the fields and the mountains, on the grain, the new wine, the olive oil and everything else the ground produces, on people and livestock, and on all the labor of your hands." (Emphasis Added).

God spoke to the Jewish people and gave them a simple message: they had become distracted, and they had forsaken their most important task. From the description provided in Haggai, the Jews were living in their completed paneled houses, while God's house remained in ruins. Yet the people were saying *"The time has not yet come to rebuild the LORD's house."* (Haggai 1:2). Why would this not be the right time? I think that verses 7–11 give us a clue: the people were preoccupied with the management of their own homes, their crops, and their livestock. This was a practical concern. The people needed food after all. But it became such a focus for them that days stretched on while the temple of God remained in ruin. God challenges them and reminds them who has the power to give them their crops and multiply their livestock. God had shut up the heavens, because of their neglect of his home, and as a result they *"planted much, but harvested little"* (Haggai 1:6).

In response, God calls them to do something rather interesting. God could have limited his message to a simple "get back to work" sort of statement. Yet God calls them to *"Give careful thought to your ways"* (v. 5 and 7). He then goes on to outline how much they had toiled, planted, and worked, and how little was being produced by their efforts. He was challenging their original assumption that it was not yet time to rebuild the Lord's home. He was calling them to consider their ways, look to the fruits of their efforts, and consider if God was blessing their current approach.

I think this passage provides us a great first step to take for ourselves. We should start by giving careful thought to our ways. This book has outlined a teaching and proclamation to the church that singles ministry and the single man and single woman can be one of the most powerful contributors to the body of Christ. We have to review our Church culture and ask whether we are inadvertently hurting our singles ministries based on false beliefs that do not align with Scripture. It has called us to repent in showing "equal concern" for all members of the body of Christ, and not being selective in which ministries we are concerned for. Lastly, it has also called single disciples to embrace this identity and calling, and to elevate ministry to the body of Christ to the top of their priorities. Now, give careful thought to your ways. Do you see in any of these points where you may have fallen short? Can you identify where you may not have honored God's Word? Can you see where you may have been influenced by or perpetuated a culture that did not uphold God's Word? And please understand that this is not directed at singles alone, but at every member of the body of Christ, for we all bear the responsibility of one another.

It is during such an assessment that having the voice of singles is necessary. What are the needs, challenges, and opportunities that our singles ministries are seeing? Ask them for their perspective, and their experience within your church. Do your singles feel that they have been equally considered? Why or why not? Do your singles believe that their ministries are "dead"? Do they believe they are overlooked when it comes to investment? Do your singles feel that your church elevates marriage above singlehood? Do they believe that a proper vision for singlehood has been promoted within their ministry and/or from the pulpit? Seek out the condition of your singles ministry, for what you are going to find is the fruit of your current ways. Consider your ways and then take stock of what you have built. This is a vital step to understanding the needs of your single brothers and sisters. If we have built ministries that are in disrepair, then we should know it, own it, and set out to correct our ways. This means giving careful thought to our ways to uncover any sinful attitudes or practices we may have enacted before. It is always so helpful to identify those attitudes and actions that do not align with God's Word, because then we can repent and correct them. Sometimes it is not overt sin, but rather the sins of omission that we must take stock of: *"If anyone, then, knows the good they ought to do and doesn't do it, it is sin for them."* (James 4:17). This is where overlooking the needs of our brothers and sisters, or not having equal concern for each other can manifest as sin for us. We know the good we ought to do, but we may find that we are not carrying it out.

Give careful thought to your ways, yes, but do not stop at simply identifying sinful attitudes or practices. Set out to lay these attitudes and practices before God, and to each other. Confession and prayer are the starting point to healing, as James 5:16 says: *"Therefore confess your sins to each other and pray for each other so that you may be healed. The prayer of a righteous person is powerful and effective."* I believe that when we thoughtfully consider our ways, humble ourselves before God, acknowledge our sins, and commit to prayer, then our hearts will be prepared for the next step.

Action Step 2: Bring the Community Together

Haggai 1:12

12Then Zerubbabel son of Shealtiel, Joshua son of Jozadak, the high priest, and the whole remnant of the people obeyed the voice of the LORD their God and the message of the prophet Haggai, because the LORD their God had sent him. And the people feared the LORD.

The power of community cannot be understated. The message concerning the powers and crowns for singles is a high calling that requires the encouragement, spurring, discipleship, and commitment that all ministry requires. This is a difficult challenge for a person to take on individually, but when they have a community behind them, they are empowered through the strength of the Holy Spirit working through the collective faith of the people. This power should never be discounted. As such, we see that when the message of God reaches Haggai, he does not only direct his message to the leaders of the community but to *the whole remnant of the people*" (v. 12). Collectively they gathered to hear the message of Haggai, and collectively they *obeyed the voice of the LORD their God and the message of the prophet Haggai*" (v. 12).

To apply this lesson to our current context, I believe it benefits the whole body to be gathered together to listen to this message about rebuilding our singles ministries. I am familiar with the power of this, because through my years as a Christian I have seen ministers preach similar messages from the pulpit to the benefit of various other ministries. I have seen churches raise their contributions, I have seen volunteers stirred to action, I have seen spiritually dormant disciples come alive to respond to the needs presented. What if a call to action that has benefited so many ministries in the past was made on behalf of your singles ministry? The work of building ministry is a collective endeavor. We do not get stronger campus, teen or married ministries without the collective strength and encouragement of one another. We give and are given to. This is the power of community. We often respond in incredible ways as a community when a need is presented, and more importantly, when we are called to the higher standards of God's Word. When the Jews *"obeyed the voice of the LORD their God"* (v. 12) it was because they first were presented this Word. A great place to start is by gathering your church together, and presenting this need, presenting God's Word, and allowing the community a chance to respond with the power of the Holy Spirit.

Once we have the power of community, along with the Holy Spirit who is at work within us, we can then engage in the next step.

Call to Action Step 3: Rebuild

Haggai 1:13-15

[13]Then Haggai, the LORD's messenger, gave this message of the LORD to the people: "I am with

you," declares the LORD. [14]So the LORD stirred up the spirit of Zerubbabel son of Shealtiel, governor of Judah, and the spirit of Joshua son of Jozadak, the high priest, and the spirit of the whole remnant of the people. They came and began to work on the house of the LORD Almighty, their God, [15]on the twenty-fourth day of the sixth month.

The collective response of the community in obedience to God's Word, was met with an immediate encouragement from God *"I am with you"* (v. 13). Those simple words were then backed by God's action, as the Scripture tells us that God stirred the spirit of the governor, the high priest, and of *"the whole remnant of the people"* (v. 14). With this stirred spirit, the people abandoned their focus on self, and got back to the work of rebuilding the house of the LORD Almighty, their God, once again.

It is my sincere belief that as disciples of Christ, we desire to see God's Church built up. We may slip into self-focus, or selfishness (or is it just me?), but when we are presented with needs through Scripture and called to action, I have found that disciples are more often willing to sacrifice, serve, and give in powerful ways. This itself helps engage all the various gifts and members of the collective body of Christ so that we can see Christ formed a little more in our communities, and a little more in us as well, to the glory of God. What if this power was called upon for the sake of our single brothers and sisters?

This is where our third action step takes us: we must commit to rebuild our singles ministries. Perhaps your singles ministry is not in the state of disrepair that the temple of God was in, and praise God if that is the case. It often means that you have invested in your singles along the way. You can endeavor to make sure that the proper Scriptural vision for your singles continues to be taught. You can also seek out any practical needs that may exist and find ways to meet them as a larger body. Continue to build on the strong foundation.

For other singles ministries, there may be quite a bit of disrepair to the point where you must rebuild from the ground up. That is okay as well. God knows how to give strength, vision, purpose, and hope. He gives life to that which some may declare as dead. Together as the body of Christ, and with the working of the Holy Spirit within us, we can embark in building up our singles to be examples of the powers and crowns ministries that God envisions, not only so they will be benefitted themselves, but so that they may be a blessing to the entire body of Christ, and a light to the community of singles in this world.

Many reading this step about rebuilding your singles ministry may think that the call to action is simply to raise contributions and hire the right people to head up this ministry. This may be possible in some churches who are blessed with an abundance of resources, and even then, it will still be a collaborative effort in partnership with the larger body. However, for most churches, the money to hire a full-time staff couple with the experience that a singles ministry would necessitate is just not going to be there. If God has blessed your church with money, then certainly use that tool to build your singles. But if your church has not been blessed with financial resources, you must assess what God has blessed you with instead. Sitting within our community of churches are amazing disciples filled with the Holy Spirit. If you take an assessment of the disciples in your church community, you will find those who have had previous ministry experience, have been on church plantings, have led ministries, and have mentored and raised up leaders. This is invaluable experience that is needed to rebuild a ministry! Consider the number of married couples who came out of our singles, and who lived abundantly sacrificial and ministry-focused lives as singles. These are the people you will want to join your rebuilding efforts. Just as singles are often shoulder tapped to go help with teen or campus ministries, lets return the favor and send the experienced ministry builders in our communities back their way. The lack of money should not be an excuse. It just means that we need to use our other resources, and God has provided us plenty, especially his Holy Spirit. Haggai described how God stirred the spirits of the people towards the work of rebuilding the temple. The Holy Spirit can do the same for us. If we have anything in our communities, it is Christians who have sacrificed for the Gospel in many incredible ways. You may find that with the help of the Holy Spirit, these disciples will be found more than willing to respond to the calling to help rebuild this ministry.

One commentary, in reference to the passage from 1 Corinthians 4:20 quoted at the start of this chapter, expressed the meaning behind this passage in the following way:

> "The kingdom of Christ does not consist in paltry eloquence, in great, swelling words of vanity, but in the power of the Holy Spirit, exerted through the Word upon the hearts of men. Where this power rules, there is the kingdom of the Savior."[1]

It is time to set words aside and commit to action. My prayer is that the power of the Holy Spirit will be made manifest in our response to this call to rebuild our ministries. The Word upon our hearts stirring us to action and becoming the catalyst for the Holy Spirit to manifest his power. Let us listen intently for God's Word and voice to spur us towards action and let us seek to please God with the Word firmly set upon our hearts. From this, my prayer is that we will see the kingdom of the Savior rule in great power over us.

More can be written about rebuilding our singles ministries, but I will simply state an obvious fact: the work must be a collaboration with the singles in your congregation. We

1 Kretzmann, Paul E. Ph. D., D. D. "Commentary on 1 Corinthians 4". "Kretzmann's Popular Commentary". https://www.studylight.org/commentaries/eng/kpc/1-corinthians-4.html. 1921-23.

can sometimes place this type of work in the hands of leaders and exclude those who we are calling to be owners. We need the owners to be part of the conversation. This collaboration will allow for there to be ownership on behalf of the singles, as well as the church community. A collaboration like this may also mean that it would be prudent to have single leaders represented on your leadership teams as well. Together with the Holy Spirit, the singles ministries in your church can be rebuilt, and your singles will elevate their unique gifts in ways you have not seen before, all to the glory of God. But we must commit to this rebuilding.

Not a Matter of Talk, but of Power

The beautiful strength of disciples of Christ is how we engage in putting God's Word into practice. When we are cut to the heart, we do not let matters remain as mere talk. We are instead spurred to action. Paul spoke powerful truth when he said, *"For the kingdom of God is not a matter of talk but of power."* (1 Corinthians 4:20). Within its context, it was about weighing the power of individuals who were spreading ungodly influences within the church in Corinth. It is the belief of this writer that we are not facing ungodly people preaching falsehoods within our churches, but nevertheless falsehoods have cropped up in our culture and our singles have suffered the results of their fruit. My hope is to uproot these false ideas and cut off their power and influence so that we can build up our single brothers and sisters to be their most for God. But this hope will require us to be congregations that are not mere talk, but of power. Congregations that seek to elevate God's Word and correct ourselves in areas where we are falling short of God's expectations.

By giving careful thought to our ways, by bringing the community together to hear God's voice, and by calling ourselves to action to build our singles ministries, we can ensure that we are allowing God's power to be demonstrated, and ensure that we are not just talking, but doing! This is God's call to action.

CHAPTER FIVE

Old-Fashioned Tent Revivals

We have thus far discussed the idea of singles ministry in theory, but aside from a few personal examples, there is not much represented in the form of practice. This is where we turn to a few practical examples of singles who submitted the single stage of their life to God, submitted their powers and crowns, and the fruit that this generated. In this chapter, we will explore the singles experiences of Angela Williams, Angela Perry, Martin Ellis, and Rosa Alejandro. While this sampling of experiences is by no means exhaustive, I believe their stories illustrate the real opportunities we have with a singles ministry oriented around having powers and crowns submitted to God. I pray these stories, examples, and convictions will be a spark for the Spirits work inside of you. But before we hear from these modern-day examples, let us look first to the examples of single men and women in Scripture.

Kings, Prophets, Evangelists and More!

This book has spoken much about an ideology against singlehood that treats the single stage of life as a nuisance, and as an unpreferable state. Misery and loneliness accompany it, and spiritual malaise and aloofness are its fruits. This book has stood to challenge these ideas as being unbiblical. The single stage of life is one to pursue, construct, inspire, and lead. This vision of singlehood is found throughout Scripture. In a recent conversation with John Reus, an evangelist of the One Miami Church in Miami, Florida, John helped me to see something that was so obvious yet remained obscure to me until the moment he mentioned it. As a single man, I often looked to the examples of Jesus and Paul for inspiration, and I think for good reason. But as John pointed out to me that day, Scripture is full of such examples. What I realized was that in my own reading of Scripture, I perhaps assumed marital status when no assumption was necessary. For example, Paul's traveling companions throughout his various missionary journeys: Barnabas, Mark, Silas, and Timothy. Is it safer to assume that these were single men traveling with Paul, or that these were men who abandoned their families to travel the world with Paul?

Is it not odd that in two letters written to Timothy, there is no mention of a wife? Or consider that Paul seems to allude to himself and Barnabas as being the only ones not exercising rights of apostles, including the rights to bring with them a believing wife (1 Corinthians 9:5-6). I wish to be clear; I am not stating definitively that these men were all single. It is not wise to be strong in assertions where Scripture is silent, but that argument runs both ways: assuming these men to be married lacks precedence. Does our perspective about singlehood change if we consider the possibility that these were single men using their freedom to preach the Gospel around the world with Paul, another single man? We know that the prophet Jeremiah was commanded explicitly not to marry (Jeremiah 16:2) and was thus a single man standing up for the truth of God in an apostate Israel. Is there something to be learned from the boldness of a man who had to speak truth to power, and was constantly under the threat of harm for doing so? Or what of the prophet Daniel, who is never said to have married (and being a court officer taken as a slave, the specter of castration is at least within the realm of possibilities)? Are there lessons to be learned from Anna the prophetess who after being widowed, committed her devotion to God and worshipped him at the temple day and night? What can we glean from Lydia's service to the community of widows? Is there something to be learned from the fact that David was crowned King of Israel as a single man, or that Joseph ascended to second in command over Egypt while still single? The point is that we can look to Scripture and see examples of single men and women who devoted themselves to God, and served as prophets, rulers and servants of the Highest. There were many others who were married but accomplished great things in the single stage of their lives. Far from being a waiting period for them, it was a building period. It was a time of boldness and facing challenges, and God elevated them through their faith. I include these examples, as a starting place for your own exploration. Consider what you can learn from the ways these individuals used the single stage of their lives for God. Consider what powers and crowns they needed to submit to God, and the results of their submission. Then consider how these examples can be applied to your own life. What powers and crowns can you submit to be used for the kingdom of God, and what can he accomplish through your faith? When we take into consideration the examples of what people were able to accomplish as single men and women in Scripture, we may also begin to see how our current "waiting period" philosophy for singles ministry is a huge waste.

Yet there is an additional category of singlehood that we have not talked much about. For this we turn to Matthew 19:12:

> "For there are eunuchs who were born that way, and there are eunuchs who have been made eunuchs by others—**and there are those who choose to live like eunuchs for the sake of the kingdom of heaven.** The one who can accept this should accept it." (Emphasis added)

This statement comes after Jesus nullified the divorce certificate that was allowed under the law of Moses. After describing the permanency of marriage, Jesus' disciples openly state that it would be better not to marry. Jesus' response is the quote provided above. He mentions that there are people out there who were born eunuchs, and others who were made eunuchs, but there is also a third category. This is a category of people who are not eunuchs in a corporal sense, that is they have not been castrated, but still choose to live as if they were. And why would anyone choose this for themselves? In Jesus' words "...for the sake of the kingdom of heaven." This is an incredible statement. It is certainly not a command, but Jesus is stating that there will be those in our fellowships who will commit to a lifetime of celibacy to commit the entirety of their being to the kingdom of heaven. It was why the prophetess Anna could worship day and night at the temple, and why Jeremiah could so freely prophecy himself into prison without the concern of looking after a family. Christianity has a long-standing historical tradition of righteous men and women who committed to celibacy for the sake of the kingdom. The reason for this is that the kingdom of heaven is worth sacrificing even our sexual impulses for. That is a difficult concept to grasp in a culture like ours that idolizes sex, but this idea of chosen celibacy comes from Jesus himself. Why do I bring this up? Because perhaps there are brothers and sisters out there who would very well like to follow this path, but do not find themselves in a church culture that is receptive to it. We need to normalize this path for our singles once again. If someone wishes to commit themselves to a period or a lifetime of celibacy for the kingdom of God, then as their family, we should make sure there is ample opportunity for these disciples to serve. This is not meant to make celibacy prescriptive, but simply to allow this practice to return. I suspect there could be some Paul's and Anna's sitting dormant in our churches right now with the gift to evangelize and prophecy. Let us go wake them.

This is a brief devotional that I hope will be used as a starting point to begin studying what the single stage of life can be for you. These biblical examples, and teachings are meant to ground us in the truth about what this stage of life can be. But it is often helpful to hear stories of what the submission of powers and crowns can look like in our current day in time. To this end, we will now turn towards some modern-day examples of disciples who have served in both small and big ways for the sake of the kingdom of God. I believe these examples are just small glimpses into what can be the spirit and essence of your singles ministry.

Powers and Crowns at Work Today

Angela Perry was baptized into the Southern Cities region of the Boston Church of Christ singles ministry in 1998 and described a group that was excited to be serving God. "It just looked like they wanted to live life to the full." Angela described. "It looked like they were enjoying their experience in the church and that they were giving their all." Yet beginning in 2003, funding for the church began to dry up and the church needed to reorganize. The singles ministry lost their paid staff, as the church reeled from the lack of funding and the subsequent reallocation of resources. It reached a point a few years later where the once vibrant, joyful ministry was disheartened, discouraged, and disengaged. "It was very disheartening and discouraging. Apathy started to settle in across the church and especially the singles…The men and even the women, we were kind of giving up. No one was leading the charge on any real capacity and so there was no clear vision."

At this point, Angela devised a plan. A small step of faith that she hoped would spark the ministry back to life. "I remember in my heart I felt like 'oh my gosh, something has to be done', and so I approached another pretty proactive single sister and we got lunch together. I just wanted to brainstorm how we could initiate spurring the brothers on. The light had gone out from their eyes, that's what it felt like."

The plan was simple. They would gather the brothers in their ministry for a brunch and use the time together to jump start the ministry. "We mobilized a band of sisters and we hosted a huge brunch, invited the brothers, but our goal and our premise was to let them know that we were behind them. That we were ready to rally as their cheerleaders! Then we just pulled out some calendars and we started planning and forming ideas through their lead. And from that brunch, we established a singles planning committee that went on to revive the spiritual well-being and strength of our ministry, slowly but surely."

This brunch helped galvanize the group in a time of severe discouragement and it sparked the light in both brothers and sisters alike. "We just kind of did what Nehemiah principally did. We prayed and we met the threat... [and] God used us to spur things on." Angela explained.

This theme of initiating and being the small spark that helps get ministries moving is a real opportunity. Rosa Alejandro was baptized as a campus student and spent her early years of singlehood working with the youth ministry in Miami. She met her future husband and was married a little over a year after they started dating. Unfortunately, as a few years passed, spiritual challenges began to set in. "We were married, had two beautiful boys together, but unfortunately after four years he decided to leave God, leave the Church." About a year later, she also decided to leave the church as well, and a short while later, they ended up divorcing. For two years thereafter Rosa lived in the world as a single woman but was called back to God after an experience helped her to see how far she had strayed. After studying the Bible with some sisters in the church she was restored. "I was like the prodigal daughter who came back to God." Rosa described with great joy. Only now she was navigating new waters.

"I was restored, I was in the singles ministry, my children are small still (5 and 9 years-old) and I'm a single mom." The singles ministry she was restored to was also going through a transition, and although it had some oversight, it did not have any direct leadership. Rosa desired to help get some fellowship opportunities going for the ministry, so she decided to initiate and organize a kayaking trip. "I was pitching this to some sisters, and they were like 'Yeah, that sounds great!'"

So, Rosa began coordinating the event, using social media and creating a flyer to get the word out. The result was that a singles ministry struggling through a transition, turned up in great numbers for an encouraging fellowship opportunity at the park.

"I thought if God put it in my heart, then I should do it. I thought that this would encourage people, and I was sure people would join in, and they did." Rosa explained.

The easy thing to do when a ministry is going through challenges is to disengage. But this is the opportunity to put the powers and crowns to work. To take your own experience, your talents, your skills, and your heart for God, and use these assets to be a spark for your ministry.

"Do what God puts on your heart." Rosa implored. "Think about what talent or gift you have to contribute and don't be afraid to use it. Don't wait for somebody to tell you to use it, because they might not even know you have it. Just put it out there and do it. If everybody did their part, this ministry would be unstoppable."

Rosa desired to serve in her singles ministry with the time and opportunities she had while also navigating her life as a restored single mom with two boys. Rosa would go on to start hosting her Bible talk group in her home and helped organize a plan to make sure that any kids present would be taken care of. "I never wanted any parents to feel burdened not to come and bring their kids. So, I was like 'Well, I'll take care of them… we'll take turns'… almost like an unofficial Kingdom Kids class."

For Rosa, initiating in ministry as a single mom was a way for her to take the experience and power of parenthood and use that for God's kingdom. "As a parent you can love in a different way, more deeply. You have to take advantage of all the maturity that you have. All the experience, the talent, the skills. Not to tire yourself out, and be unwise, but really just to be your brother's keeper, and use your talent and gift for what God puts on your heart."

This powerful love and experience of parenthood is a real power and crown that can be used to bring glory to God and to be a light for his kingdom.

Martin Ellis was also a restored disciple who had experienced the difficulty of divorce while away from the church until God called him back home. His experience was a bit unique as he was restored in a married's group, and initially remained with this married's group despite the local congregation having a singles ministry. This was a period where the singles ministry in this church community did not have a defined singles leader and was doing its best to support its own initiatives. "I didn't really get a good foundation with singles established, and I didn't know any different." Martin described. After a sister encouraged/challenged him to engage with the singles ministry in his local fellowship, Martin took his initial steps to engage with the singles ministry. But as he would admit, it was challenging for him to get into the flow of the ministry. There were monthly devotionals, but the group was split with roughly 2/3rd of the singles in marrieds Bible talks, and 1/3rd in dedicated singles groups. This made for an atmosphere that felt disjointed.

Martin would later transfer his job over to Arizona:

"Arizona was set up with all singles in one zone… We're in single Bible talks, weekly discipling times, confessing sins. It was healthy." After a year in Arizona, Martin would end up moving to Boston where he saw many strengths in the singles ministry, but saw an opportunity to contribute in building up the discipling relationships with the men. Martin observed that many of the men he spoke with or interacted with were stuck in their careers. They were not aspiring for greater achievements in life or setting goals. So, he got involved, using his own experience as an executive in the corporate world to help spur his fellow brothers and sisters towards greater career advancement.

"I taught a workshop with a single sister about growing your employment, making yourself more employable." The workshop seemed to resonate with many around the church body that Martin, along with a group of older singles, ended up putting on the workshop for the larger church community.

"The singles were giving back to the body, and that blew everybody away." Martin explained.

But perhaps Martin's greatest influence is in his personal relationships. When Martin arrived in Boston, he was awaiting a promised job that was delayed in coming. As a result, Martin found himself unemployed, with a daughter in college, living in an expensive city and needing to pay rent. Despite Martin reaching the executive level heights of corporate America, he became an example for other brothers by taking on a side gig driving Uber, and absolutely thriving in it. Martin described how some other brothers who were not presently working were hesitant to do something like Uber, because they believed that money could not be made doing so. He proved them wrong. "I said, 'I'm doing Uber, and I want to show you guys how much money you can make. I was making with Uber $8,000 to $9,000 a month. Had it down to a science." When the pandemic began, he had to pivot. "I switched to Instacart. Making a little less now, making $6,000 a month. Fewer hours. Where I can do 18 hour days if I had to [with Uber], with Instacart I'm limited to 10 hours." What was incredible about this was how much Martin could use this momentary setback to not just encourage the brothers to not take their own setbacks lying down, but he also used this new position with Uber to spread the Gospel, sharing his faith as he went. This led to five fruitful Bible studies where men got to hear the Gospel message, all to the glory of God.

Yet Martin remains focused on the greater goal of spurring the brothers to achieve more in their lives. "I looked at brothers and I said, 'they're underemployed', and here's my biggest hook for everybody as a disciple: you have a secret weapon. It's called character… you know how to be humble. You know how to apologize. You know how to work as if you're working for the Lord." According to Martin, this character is attractive to employers who are looking for people they can trust and build their business on.

In addition to Martin's desire to help men succeed in their careers, he has also used his power and crown of organization to meet practical needs. Along with another brother in the church, the two built a snow removal team, had the brothers in their singles ministry contribute to buying a snow blower, and on snowy nights, they head out to the single sister's homes to clear the snow from their driveways. "We went out and bought a beautiful snow blower, and the ramps and everything to throw it in my truck. So, we can keep it at one of the single sister's houses, and at first snow, that morning, we get over there at 6:00 a.m., pull out that snow blower, and we can do a driveway every 30 minutes." The hope is to grow this so that they can have two teams of brothers going.

"Every ministry should have a moving team. Every ministry should have a snow removal team… every ministry should have a cooking team… It gives people something to volunteer for, and all of a sudden you now have an organized Men's ministry." One that is living out the directive from Galatians 6:10 which says: *"Therefore, as we have opportunity, let us do good to all people, especially to those who belong to the family of believers."*

Old-Fashioned Tent Revivals

Angela Perry, Martin Ellis, and Rosa Alejandro's practical examples of taking initiative and ownership of their ministries are encouraging, but there is even greater power when a group of singles comes together with this same heart and spirit of initiative and ownership. It is no small matter when individual Christians start taking ownership of their part in the ministry. In this, we see the passage from

Ephesians 4:15-16 begin to manifest:

> "[15]Instead, speaking the truth in love, we will grow to become in every respect the mature body of him who is the head, that is, Christ. [16]From him the whole body, joined and held together by every supporting ligament, grows and builds itself up in love, **as each part does its work**." (Emphasis added).

It is this collective call for "each part" to do its work where the direction, culture, and heart of a group can begin to be changed and transformed. Back in 2010, Angela Williams attended a midweek service in the Coastal Region of the Los Angeles Church of Christ led by Marco Pellizerri. Marco and his wife Michelle had been hired to lead the singles ministry in the Coastal Region, where Angela attended. Much like Angela Perry and Rosa Alejandro's experiences, this singles ministry was going through a difficult time.

"At that time, ministry was dead. There were some people who were sharing their faith and reaching out, but it was just a real dead time." Angela recounted.

Marco used this midweek to inspire the group to get back to the basics, getting grounded in the Word, and in many ways, returning to their first love. God used this lesson to stir the hearts of the disciples. As Angela recounted, people were moved by this message. After the lesson, people were going up to Marco to confess their sins, and from this initial midweek service, the singles ministry started taking steps together to draw closer to God. As the midweeks progressed, little embers began to ignite into living flames in the hearts of the disciples. People just naturally started studying the Bible with others, and people just started showing up. What was first described as a dead ministry, began to stir to life, culminating in experiences that Angela Williams would describe as "Old fashioned tent revivals".

"We [read] a book together, and every midweek that we came together we had a lesson from the book usually taught by Marco, but also by the interns or leaders that he was raising up, and it was so simple. God bonded us. Like we just became this family… The synergy of having the singles all together, something about that…" The results of these midweek classes was an incredible outpouring of grace as God added to their numbers those who were being saved.

"One of the things I loved about that was as a result, there was a lot of fruit that summer. We had a lot of people that were restored, got baptized." Angela explained.

As that summer progressed, Angela described how they began organizing the group to share these short life testimonies, dubbed "transformonials" at their services, so that others could hear the amazing transformations that God was working in the lives of the disciples.

"People were just chomping at the bit to get up, and it became this thing, it became part of our culture. Just having someone get up there and share how they used to be a part of a gang, and how they had killed someone and they just got out of prison, and now they're a Christian…It felt like God's Spirit was just really moving… [It] was pretty much constant. Hearing people surrendering their life to God over and over again… everybody was from some sort of different background. They had different crowns, you know? Whether their crown was a Middle Eastern Muslim background, we had a lot of single moms who come from hard marriages, we had a lot of people from all different [backgrounds]… watching that weekly was powerful… It was a manifestation of just the Gospel at work, and God's hand at work."

God worked powerfully in Angela Williams personal ministry as well, as she described God sending her into ripe harvest fields.

"So many people came to study, it was like this flood of women out of nowhere. Literally! There were so many people… I was in more Bible studies than I could shake a stick at!.. I think that was the biggest thing that I remember God doing was just bringing in a harvest. And I think, honestly, he was just blessing faith."

Angela Williams ended up interning within the singles ministry, and in time would be named a Women's Ministry Leader as a single woman, the first single woman to serve in that role in over 30 years.

The singles ministry in the Coastal Region grew from 120 disciples to over 200 disciples in just a few years, with one year seeing God bring an incredible 32 souls to the waters of baptisms. It all started with a midweek lesson where truth was spoken in love and was followed by each part doing its work as Ephesians 4:15-16 describes.

A very similar story was also told by Angela Perry in the Boston Church of Christ. After her initial surprise calendar meeting that helped spur her singles ministry to action, Angela also bore witness to a ministry revival under the leadership of a newly hired singles ministry couple, Larry and Kim Reed.

"You know, they came in and they just saw hurting people, and for a year all Larry preached about was love. Literally, like every message was love, love, love. God loves you, we love you, feel loved, be loved, love, love, love." Angela Perry explained.

While Larry and Kim preached love and displayed it in their personal ministry, Larry was also planting seeds of a vision for the future. In addition to preaching love, Larry also encouraged the singles that they could accomplish anything they wanted as a ministry.

"The singles will lead the church, and the singles can lead the church, and the singles should lead the church." This was Larry's message, as Angela Perry recounted.

When Larry arrived, there were only 2 single men in leadership positions, so Larry got to work raising up and training men to lead. The humble group of 2 grew to 15.

"He just poured himself into them out of love. Believed in them. Gave them a vision and just really expected us to have a God-honoring life, both inside and outside of the church. That's what he and Kim tried to instill to help us to embrace and recognize our spiritual worth and our spiritual value as a single person in the church. They pushed that, they spoke that, they believed that." Angela Perry described.

The investment in loving the group and inspiring them would soon pay off. The singles ministry set a goal to lead the church in baptisms for the year and pursued the goal by faith. It was an ambitious goal, particularly in a city with a large and thriving campus ministry. "[Larry] was just like, this is going to be an exciting ministry that you're going to want to bring your friends to. He just kept saying that: a loving, safe, validating ministry… and he was living it, and showing us… He and Kim kept speaking 'You know what? You guys can prominently influence the church through your spiritual impact, evangelism, talents, abilities, leadership skills… your steadfast love for God, like [they] just kept pushing it, talking it, saying it. And I think we just started believing it."

This belief, vision and investment in the singles ministry stirred the hearts of the disciples who set out to live out this vision, and God blessed their efforts. By God's grace, the singles ministry there in Boston went on to lead the church in baptisms, edging out their campus ministry by one baptism that year. To be clear, this type of competition or sharing of baptism numbers is not meant to emphasize the numbers, but the baptisms. There can be an unhealthy attachment to numbers, and rivalry can certainly turn down unhealthy paths. That is not what we should draw from this. This is not about whether singles ministry is better than campus ministry, or vice versa. It is about the glory that was brought to God. Disciples were inspired to share their faith in ways that perhaps they had not been before, and the result was more people hearing the Gospel and more people being reached for God. Angela Perry would also go on to be named a Women's Ministry Leader in Boston as a single woman as well, all to the glory of God.

Both Angela Williams and Angela Perry's stories share some commonalities, but the one that stands out to me is how both Marco and Michelle Pellizerri in LA, and Larry and Kim Reed in Boston believed in the singles ministry and imparted that belief to them. As a result, both of these singles ministries were taken from places of former discouragement, to impressive heights and manifestations of God's grace. Not every church community will have the resources to hire a ministry couple, but that is also severely missing the point. These two ministry couples were conduits of something bigger. Both the Pellizerri's and Reed's communicated to the singles in their churches what God saw in them. That is the point. Not only did they communicate what God saw in them, they showed that they believed in this vision with their actions. When singles see themselves the way God sees them and see within their lives the opportunities God has provided for them, miracles can happen. When this happens, then we have aligned ourselves with the truth of Scripture. Without lies to tangle the Spirit's work inside us, what can we now achieve? This is the opportunity when we unlock these dormant powers and crowns for the glory of God. These stories show how God can work when faith is placed in him, and ministries are stirred to action. What will your story be? What can you accomplish for God? What can your singles ministry become if you believe and invest in them? What can your powers and crowns produce for the glory of God in this world? There are many more opportunities to explore, and my hope and prayer is that these few stories will help spark your imagination and encourage you to fix your attention towards the work of building up your singles ministry.

CONCLUSION

Thoughts and Prayers

As I reflect on the contents of this book, I am reminded of the almost 2000 years that the Church has existed. It is incredible to think of all the challenges the Church has faced throughout history, and how it has persevered through them all. The church is a resilient group because it is the body of Christ. It is no ordinary, physical, and temporal body, it is a supernatural, spiritual, and eternal one. It is because of this that John can proclaim so boldly that *"The world and its desires pass away, but whoever does the will of God lives forever."* (1 John 2:17). Therefore, we do not invest in the passing mists of our times, but in the eternal ministration of his heavenly kingdom.

This book presents a perspective that our single brothers and sisters have not always had the full benefit of our collective support and concern. I believe it is time that we as a community of believers take a step back and consider how we have been building this ministry and consider new ways forward. Some congregations will be further along than others, and some may not see the issues reported in this book at all. I am grateful for this and hope to learn from the victories and achievements of these singles ministries. However, many churches boast a singles ministry that deal with the lack of vision, the conflicting cultural values, the lack of investment, and lack of equal concern that this book has discussed. It is for us to be honest with where we are at and commit to making the changes that will elevate our congregations. This should not discourage us, but rather fill us with excitement! We are discovering ways that we can grow in our Christlikeness and are being given an opportunity to build the very dwelling place where God lives! Furthermore, I believe our singles can truly accomplish greater things for God than we have seen before. What we have built so far has placed a ceiling on our single brothers and sisters that should not exist. As such, it has not allowed us to see the full extent of their contributions, or the full capacity of their abilities. Where singles have thrived, we have seen incredible examples of generous giving, of commitment to ministry, of evangelism, of church plantings, of various gifts, talents, powers, and crowns being given over for the sake of building the body of Christ. We believe those are not the exceptions, but truly the biproduct of what the single stage of life is supposed to be within the Church.

My hope and prayer is that a book like this will allow us to look at our ministry building approach with fresh eyes, and to find ways to build up the body of Christ to be even stronger. We are our best when the collective body is allowed to thrive, and each individual member has avenues to serve to the best of their abilities and are called to live by the very standards and callings outlined by God's Word. My prayer is also for singles to embrace this Biblical definition of singlehood. To stop seeing their singlehood as defining what they lack, and their worth as being tied to marriage. To be a single man or woman for God is to have God himself, and as God states through his Word, it means to have a unique opportunity for undivided devotion that will only last while you are single. Be it 1 year or a lifetime, this opportunity of undivided devotion to the affairs of the Lord is an adventure, a calling, and an opportunity like no other. So where will your faith take you? And what will you build for your God with this opportunity? Truly, your faith is the limit.

Addressing the Needs, Challenges and the Road Ahead

While this book has been focused on setting a spiritual vision for our singles ministries, we must not turn a blind eye to the very real physical, emotional and spiritual needs, and challenges that our single brothers and sisters have been experiencing. It is true that singles can struggle with loneliness and isolation as well as with the disappointment of dreams and hopes not coming true. As it reads in Proverbs 13:12 "Hope deferred makes the heart sick, but a longing fulfilled is a tree of life." For our singles who desire marriage, there have been many hopes deferred, and this scriptural principle rings true. They are not unspiritual for these deferred hopes making their hearts sick. They are hoping for that longing fulfilled that is a tree of life, and this desire is powerful one. We can certainly do what we can to help support our single brothers and sisters who desire marriage to find a great partner in Christ. But we must acknowledge that this hope deferred does have impact on our ministries, and we cannot overlook the pain that some of our singles feel as they experience loneliness, loss of hope, and in some cases a loss of faith. We also cannot overlook the bitterness that these deferred hopes can cause in the hearts of our brothers and sisters.

One thing to understand is that depression and anxiety can come hand and hand with these feelings of disappointment, and many of our single brothers and sisters struggle with these challenges. This can often drive the isolation mentioned before. The pandemic has amplified these challenges, driving further isolation, and the results have been felt by many singles ministries (indeed no one has been spared by its effects).

Other needs and challenges certainly exist, and as you take Action Step 1 from chapter four, you will want to explore what they are. The needs and challenges will be different in each congregation, which is why doing such an assessment will be important. This will help you have a complete picture of your ministry as you set out to build.

It is true that any grouping of Christians will have their needs and challenges. This is not specific to our single brothers and sisters. We have already outlined before how teen and campus ministries are resource intensive and require the investment of staff. Marriage relationships need incredible amounts of input and sustenance, and many senior ministers and elders can find much of their time is spent in ministering to the married couples of the church. Singles have their own particular needs and challenges, and I believe that we have everything we need to meet these needs, overcome these challenges, and build singles ministries that thrive. By looking at the singles ministry with the same concern as any other ministry, we can then look for the Holy Spirit to prompt the hearts of individual members to engage and help build. This will be a collective effort as all ministry is, and both singles and the churches they are a part of will need to take ownership of the work that needs to be done to build up stronger.

As was outlined in the introduction, the number of singles in this world is growing and has been growing for quite some time. We have an opportunity to proclaim the Gospel to this segment of the population and welcome them into ministries that are thriving, spirit-filled, and abounding in faith. There is no reason that we cannot build these types of ministries, but it requires vision, conviction, faith, and the work of the body. God can do amazing things through us, but are we willing to commit ourselves to the work? I believe that as followers of Christ, we are more than willing, and he will bless all our efforts to align ourselves to his Word, to show equal concern for one another, and to build his body stronger for his glory.

My Final Requests to You

As I bring the exploration of this vision to a close, I wish to ask you for a few things. First, I ask that you consider what has been discussed in this book and pray for God to grant you wisdom and his Spirit to guide you towards the actions to take next. The hope is that this does not remain a work of mere words, but that it would inspire action. For the singles reading this book, I encourage you to embrace the identity outlined in chapter 1 on the powers and crowns. Pray and reflect on this identity. This is the life you can embrace as a single disciple of Christ, and I encourage you to put the passages outlined in that chapter into practice.

Second, I ask that all who read this book commit our single brothers and sisters to prayer. Pray for singles who are struggling with the hopes deferred, who are losing heart or faith from a lack of vision, or who are simply feeling stuck in their walks with God. Pray for refreshment, for the Spirit, for their faith, and for God to illuminate the way forward. Some single disciples may feel overwhelmed at the powers and crowns calling outlined in this book as it is a lofty one, but I ask that you pray that they would be filled with courage and strength by God's Holy Spirit to see this power made manifest in their lives.

Lastly, I ask that you pray for the group that has put this book together. We are a small group of disciples who have held various leadership roles within singles ministries, and who have seen glimpses of how powerful, selfless, and generous this ministry can be. We are hoping to strengthen the body of Christ by building up this part that has been overlooked in our communities. Pray that we can spread this vision of powers and crowns, and that God will show us how we can best support a ministry dedicated to helping single disciples thrive all around the world.

Closing Prayer

Father in heaven, my prayer for this book is that it may prompt us to consider and bring attention to the needs of my single brothers and sisters, and by the faith, effort, and action of our church communities, I pray that we will see a renaissance of singles ministries. A rebirth that will spark a resurgence of evangelism and breathe new life into our churches by the power of the Holy Spirit. A rebirth that will set its focus on the worldwide spread of the Gospel, on missions, on service to the poor, on church plantings, and where our brothers and sisters will bear witness to miracles manifesting through their faith. A rebirth that will show the singles of this world the value they have as sons and daughters of the living God, as well as the incredible opportunity they have to be dedicated to him, in undivided devotion, and to receive the blessed promises of life to the full and life eternal. A rebirth that will create singles ministries full of powers and crowns submitted to Christ, for his purposes, the fruits of which will bear abundance, refreshment, and new growth for the Church around the world. I ask Father that you bring this prayer, vision, and hope to fruition. In Jesus' Holy Name I pray, whom I love, amen.

Spiritual Maturity: God's Will for Emotional Health and Healing

Without emotional intelligence and personal growth, our lives will be like the seed that fell among thorns (Luke 8:14). We will not be able to most effectively or spiritually handle life's worries, riches, and pleasures, and we will not mature. This book addresses issues that we must consider in order to live as emotionally, spiritually, and relationally mature adults. Not a quick-read book, it contains scriptures to contemplate, personal sharing, paradigm-changing insights, and reflection questions.

Chapters:
1. What You Don't Know Will Hurt You
2. My Emotional Health and Healing Journey
3. You Are Not Alone: The Power of Healing Discussion Groups
4. My Personal Heroes: Courage and Healing
5. Spiritual Foundation
6. Dig a Little Deeper: Wisdom and Emotional Health
7. Numbing the Pain and Repeating the Cycle
8. Our Fathers
9. How to Change: More than Just a Decision
Epilogue: Still a Work in Progress
Appendix l: Mental Health Disorders
Appendix ll: When to See a Professional
Appendix lll: Additional Change Models

Spiritual Transformation: Emotional Intelligence and Freedom

In a world in which interpersonal relationships have become increasingly depersonalized due to social media, the ability to identify and manage one's own emotions (as well as the emotions of others) is becoming a lost skill. This skill, known as emotional intelligence (EI), is an essential tool for disciples of Jesus, who have been tasked by God to appeal to the hearts and souls of others, in an effort to win them over and share the good news of salvation. Like other aptitudes, EI falls on a normal curve: some people have a great deal of natural EI, and others have less. Fortunately, EI can be understood, learned, and developed. In her book, Cresenda guides the reader to a better understanding of the theory and science of EI, while also providing very practical, Bible-based exercises to improve EI and progress toward greater spiritual, social, and emotional maturity. A must-have book for anyone who deals with people, which is pretty much everyone!

—Michael S. Shapiro, PhD, author of *Rejoice Always*

Chapters:

1. Take the *Emotional Intelligence 2.0* Test—Assessment Is Imperative!
2. Life without EQ
3. What is Emotional Intelligence?
4. Master Your Mind
5. The Cost of Repressing Emotions
6. God, Emotions, and Emotional Intelligence
7. The Bible on the Four Core EQ skills
8. Build Your EQ skills – The Bible on Emotional Intelligence 2.0's 66 Strategies
9. Time Line Therapy® – Transforming Our Neurology
10. Three Requisites for Mind Changes and Soul Transformations
Appendix: Is There Anything Helpful Outside God's Word?

Books for Christian Growth at www.ipibooks.com

Apologetics
Compelling Evidence for God and the Bible—Truth in an Age of Doubt, by Douglas Jacoby.
Field Manual for Christian Apologetics, by John M. Oakes.
Is There A God—Questions and Answers about Science and the Bible, by John M. Oakes.
Mormonism—What Do the Evidence and Testimony Reveal?, by John M. Oakes.
Reasons For Belief-A Handbook of Christian Evidence, by John M. Oakes.
That You May Believe—Reflections on Science and Jesus, by John Oakes/David Eastman.
The Resurrection: A Historical Analysis, by C. Foster Stanback.
When God Is Silent—The Problem of Human Suffering, by Douglas Jacoby.

Bible Basics
A Disciple's Handbook—Third Edition, Tom A. Jones, Editor.
A Quick Overview of the Bible, by Douglas Jacoby.
Be Still, My Soul—A Practical Guide to a Deeper Relationship with God, by Sam Laing.
From Shadow to Reality—Relationship of the Old & New Testament, by John M. Oakes.
Getting the Most from the Bible, Second Edition, by G. Steve Kinnard.
Letters to New Disciples—Practical Advice for New Followers of Jesus, by Tom A. Jones.
The Baptized Life—The Lifelong Meaning of Immersion into Christ, by Tom A. Jones.
The Lion Never Sleeps—Preparing Those You Love for Satans Attacks, by Mike Taliaferro.
The New Christian's Field Guide, Joseph Dindinger, Editor.
Thirty Days at the Foot of the Cross, Tom and Sheila Jones, Editors.
The Spirit—Presense & Power, Sense & Nonsense, by Douglas Jacoby.

Christian Living
According to Your Faith—The Awesome Power of Belief in God, by Richard Alawaye.
But What About Your Anger—A Biblical Guide to Managing Your Anger, by Lee Boger.
Caring Beyond the Margins—Understanding Homosexuality, by Guy Hammond.
Golden Rule Membership—What God Expects of Every Disciple, by John M. Oakes.
How to Defeat Temptation in Under 60 Seconds, by Guy Hammond.
Jesus and the Poor—Embracing the Ministry of Jesus, by G. Steve Kinnard.
How to Be a Missionary in Your Hometown, by Joel Nagel.
Like a Tree Planted by Streams of Water—Personal Spiritual Growth, G. Steve Kinnard.
Love One Another—Importance & Power of Christian Relationships, by Gordon Ferguson.
One Another—Transformational Relationships, by Tom A. Jones and Steve Brown.
Prepared to Answer—Restoring Truth in An Age of Relativism, by Gordon Ferguson.
Repentance—A Cosmic Shift of Mind & Heart, by Edward J. Anton.
Strong in the Grace—Reclaiming the Heart of the Gospel, by Tom A. Jones.
The Guilty Soul's Guide to Grace—Freedom in Christ, by Sam Laing.
The Power of Discipling, by Gordon Ferguson.
The Prideful Soul's Guide to Humility, by Tom A. Jones and Michael Fontenot.
The Way of the Heart—Spiritual Living in a Legalistic World, by G. Steve Kinnard.
The Way of the Heart of Jesus—Prayer, Fasting, Bible Study, by G. Steve Kinnard.
Till the Nets Are Full—An Evangelism Handbook for the 21st Century, by Douglas Jacoby.
Thrive—Using Psalms to Help You Flourish, by Douglas Jacoby.
Walking the Way of the Heart—Lessons for Spiritual Living, by G. Steve Kinnard.
What Happens After We Die?, by Douglas Jacoby.
What Now, God? Finding God in Transitions, by Jeanie Shaw.
When God is Silent—The Problem of Human Suffering, by Douglas Jacoby.
Values and Habits of Spiritual Growth, by Bryan Gray.

Deeper Study

A Women's Ministry Handbook, by Jennifer Lambert and Kay McKean.
After The Storm—Hope & Healing From Ezra—Nehemiah, by Rolan Dia Monje.
Aliens and Strangers—The Life and Letters of Peter, by Brett Kreider.
Crossing the Line: Culture, Race, and Kingdom, by Michael Burns.
Daniel—Prophet to the Nations, by John M. Oakes.
Exodus—Making Israel's Journey Your Own, by Rolan Dia Monje.
Exodus—Night of Redemption, by Douglas Jacoby.
Finish Strong—The Message of Haggai, Zechariah, and Malachi, by Rolan Dia Monje.
Free Your Mind—40 Days to Greater Peace, Hope, and Joy, by Sam Laing.
In Remembrance of Me—Understanding the Lord's Supper, by Andrew C. Fleming.
In the Middle of It!—Tools to Help Preteen and Young Teens, by Jeff Rorabaugh.
Into the Psalms—Verses for the Heart, Music for the Soul, by Rolan Dia Monje.
King Jesus—A Survey of the Life of Jesus the Messiah, by G. Steve Kinnard.
Jesus Unequaled—An Exposition of Colossians, by G. Steve Kinnard.
Mornings in Matthew, by Tammy Fleming.
Passport to the Land of Enough—Revised Edition, by Joel Nagel.
Prophets I—The Voices of Yahweh, by G. Steve Kinnard.
Prophets II—The Prophets of the Assyrian Period, by G. Steve Kinnard.
Prophets III—The Prophets of the Babylonian and Persion Periods, by G. Steve Kinnard.
Return to Sender—When There's Nowhere Left to God but Home, by Guy Hammond.
Romans—The Heart Set Free, by Gordon Ferguson.
Revelation Revealed—Keys to Unlocking the Mysteries of Revelation, by Gordon Ferguson.
Spiritual Leadership for Women, Jeanie Shaw, Editor.
The Call of the Wise—An Introduction and Index of Proverbs, by G. Steve Kinnard.
The Cross of the Savior—From the Perspective of Jesus..., by Mark Templer.
The Final Act—A Biblical Look at End-Time Prophecy, by G. Steve Kinnard.
The Gospel of Matthew—The Crowning of the King, by G. Steve Kinnard.
The King Jesus Translation of the New Testament, by G. Steve Kinnard.
The Letters of James, Peter, John, Jude—Life to the Full, by Douglas Jacoby.
The Lion Has Roared—An Exposition of Amos, by Douglas Jacoby.
The Mission—God and Make Disciples of All Nations, by Will and Kristen Lambert
The Recovery Journal—Jesus' Heart to Help the Hurting, by Timothy Sumerlin.
The Seven People Who Help You to Heaven, by Sam Laing.
Wildfire—How Progressive Theology is Impacting the Church, by Daren Overstreet
World Changers—The History of the Church in the Book of Acts, by Gordon Ferguson.

Marriage and Family

A Lifetime of Love—Building and Growing Your Marriage, by Al and Gloria Baird
Building Emotional Intimacy in Your Marriage, by Jeff and Florence Schachinger.
Hot and Holy—God's Plan for Exciting Sexual Intimacy in Marriage, by Sam Laing.
Faith and Finances, by Patrick Blair.
Friends & Lovers—Marriage as God Designed It, by Sam and Geri Laing.
Mighty Man of God—A Return to the Glory of Manhood, by Sam Laing.
Pure the Journey—A Radical Journey to a Pure Heart, by David and Robin Weidner.
Raising Awesome Kids—Being the Great Influence in Your Kids' Lives by Sam and Geri Laing.
Principle-Centered Parenting, by Douglas and Vicki Jacoby.
The Essential 8 Principles of a Growing Christian Marriage, by Sam and Geri Laing.
The Essential 8 Principles of a Strong Family, by Sam and Geri Laing.
Warrior—A Call to Every Man Everywhere, by Sam Laing.

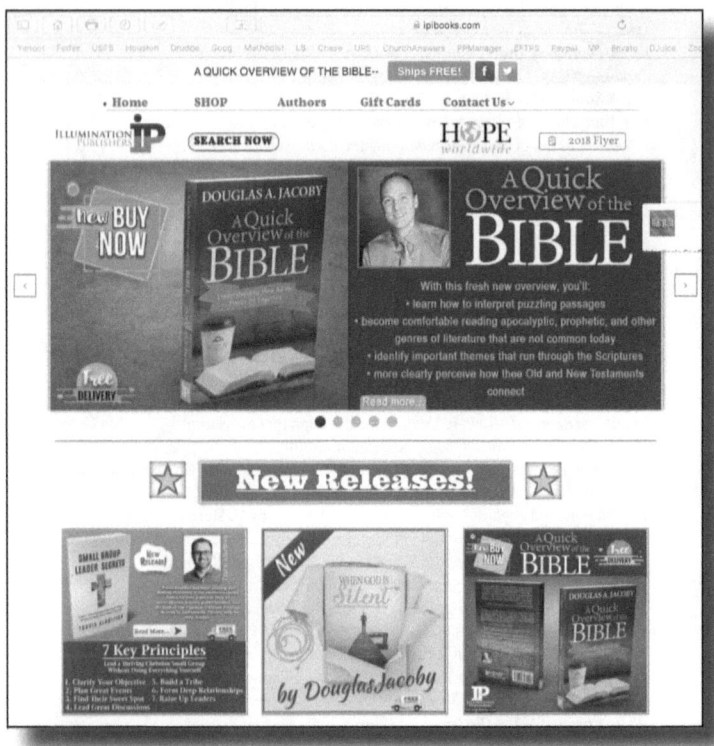

For additional books go to
www.ipibooks.com